ENGAGED MANAGEMENT

VOLUME 2

MAXIMIZING YOUR TEAM'S SALES PERFORMANCE

JOHN HANNON

PATTY,
WISHING you THE BEST
OF CAREER AND LIFE SUCCESS!

ENGAGED MANAGEMENT
VOLUME 2
MAXIMIZING YOUR TEAM'S SALES
PERFORMANCE

Jim Doyle & Associates
7711 Holiday Drive
Sarasota, FL 34231

(941) 926-7355
FAX: (941) 925-1114
john@jimdoyle.com
www.jimdoyle.com
www.doyleondemand.com

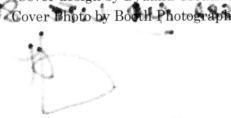

Also by John Hannon

ENGAGED MANAGEMENT
VOLUME 1
INSPIRING YOUR TEAM TO WIN

Available at:

jimdoyle.com/store-2

CONTENTS

<u>ACKNOWLEDGEMENTS</u> i

<u>FOREWORD</u> iii

<u>INTRODUCTION</u> 1

CHAPTER 1
LEADING THE TEAM

TRUE LEADERS POSSESS A BUILD-A-BENCH VISION 3

HELP YOUR TEAM FIND THEIR PASSION AND COMMITMENT .. 5

FOUR THINGS YOU MUST DO IN THE SECOND HALF OF
THE YEAR 7

A CULTURE CHANGE DOESN'T HAPPEN OVERNIGHT ... 13

INSIST THAT YOUR SELLERS LIVE UP TO THEIR
TITLE 15

WANTEPRENEURS VS. ENTREPRENEURS 19

DOES YOUR GENERAL MANAGER MAKE SALES A
PRIORITY? 22

MANAGING UP WITH YOUR GENERAL MANAGER 24

DON'T SKIP A STEP 28

YOU HAVE TO GET UP WITH THE ROOSTERS IF YOU
WANT TO SOAR WITH THE EAGLES 30

INCREASING PERFORMANCE THROUGH THE POWER OF
APPRECIATION 32

CHAPTER 2
COACHING TO WIN

EVERYONE ON THE TEAM TAKES GROUNDERS ... 35

NAVIGATING THE AGENCY AND CLIENT RELATIONSHIP ... 37

A LESSON FROM A HOT DOG STAND OWNER 39

A TOPIC THAT MUST BE ON YOUR TRAINING AGENDA .. 41

ELEVEN THINGS THAT MAKE THE DIFFERENCE 45

OH CANADA! 49

PUTTING A POSITIVE SPIN ON NEGATIVE WORDS 51

PERCEPTION IS NOT REALITY 53

THE REASON "ANY DAY" NEVER COMES FOR YOUR AE'S 55

THE ART OF TRIAL CLOSING FOR SALES SUCCESS 56

WHEN AN EXPERIENCED AE SHOOTS LOW 59

GET WITH ME AFTER THE HOLIDAYS 63

RECOVERING FROM ADVERSITY 65

CHAPTER 3
MANAGING FOR MAXIMUM PERFORMANCE

WHEN YOU WANT IT MORE THAN THEY DO IT'S TIME TO SAY GOODBYE 67

THERE'S MORE THAN ONE MANAGEMENT STYLE TO GET IMPROVED REVENUE PERFORMANCE 68

A TWIST ON MEASURING NEW BUSINESS 70

"C" MANAGERS CAN'T LEAD "A" SELLERS, BUT "A" SELLERS WILL LEAD "C" MANAGERS 72

CONVERTING OLD CLIENTS INTO NEW CLIENTS 74

DO YOU HAVE A SALES BUSINESS PLAN? 75

NOT EQUAL GIVING, BUT EQUAL SACRIFICES 78

THE SALE IS NOT COMPLETE UNTIL THE MONEY IS COLLECTED 80

WHAT IS THE MAGIC NUMBER OF REPS FOR YOUR TEAM? .. 82

DON'T BE A "CONGRATULATIONS, BUT..." MANAGER 84

ACCOUNT EXECUTIVES HAVE NEEDS 86

THERE ARE RICHES IN NICHES 87

THE POWER OF TESTIMONIALS 89

CHAPTER 4
SALES PREPARATION AND PLANNING

FIVE AREAS WHERE SALESPEOPLE NEED HELP 93

AN ANNUAL REMINDER TO FOCUS 97

A SOMETIMES OVERLOOKED REVENUE CATEGORY 100

CLOSE MORE BUSINESS WITH THE RIGHT SUIT COLOR ... 103

IS YOUR TEAM SELLING THE DRILL BIT OR THE HOLE? .. 105

LOOK PAST THE "I" IN YOUR THANK YOU 107

SELLING TO BIRTH ORDER 109

212 DEGREES 116

THE BEST TIME TO MAKE COLD CALLS 117

A COUNTER VIEW TO SILENCE AS A SALES TOOL ... 119

AN ALL-IN SALES SYSTEM 121

IT'S TIME FOR A PRESENTATION REVIEW 125

CHAPTER 5
WITHOUT CUSTOMERS YOU HAVE NO BUSINESS

IGNORING A CUSTOMER'S COMPLAINT IS A HUGE
MISTAKE 129

A SALES MAINTENANCE REMINDER 132

SIGNS AND THE MESSAGES THEY CONVEY TO
CUSTOMERS 134

THE TRUMP CARD IN ALL SALES SCENARIOS 135

ENCOURAGE YOUR SELLERS TO BE CLIENT CUPIDS .. 137

ASSUMPTIONS AND CUSTOMER SERVICE SURVEYS DO
NOT MIX 140

CHAPTER 6
FOCUS ON YOUR CAREER

THE REAL WORK BEGINS AFTER THE MEETING 143

ACTIVATE YOUR MINDSET SWITCH 146

ARE YOU PREPARING YOUR REPLACEMENT? 147

WHAT DO I DO WITH ALL OF THESE SUBSCRIPTIONS?... 151

SAYING YES BEFORE YOU SAY NO 153

HIRE SELLERS WHO BUY LOTTERY TICKETS .. 155

THREE STEPS TO TAPPING UNREALIZED POTENTIAL... 158

YOU FIND WHAT YOU'RE LOOKING FOR 160

CHANGE YOUR LICENSE PLATES 161

WHEN WAS THE LAST TIME YOU TOOK A TRUE
VACATION? 164

THE THREE PHASES OF CAREER THINKING 166

THE FINAL LESSON

MANAGEMENT BY WALKING AROUND 169

ABOUT THE AUTHOR
.... 173

EXPERIENCE DOYLE ON DEMAND
.... 175

THE LEADERS EDGE
.... 177

CONTACTS
.... 179

ACKNOWLEDGEMENTS

So Grateful…

For my wife Bridget and children Madison, Cara and Evan, and their consistent patience with the pursuit of my passion. They are more understanding than they should be of my late-night office hours and sometimes unforgiving travel schedule.

To Robin Renna, the architect of the *Engaged Management* series. She's the timekeeper of this project and the quiet but firm voice when I miss a deadline.

To the Jim Doyle & Associates clients, partners, and friends. You have welcomed me into your businesses and lives. Your success drives the motivation for sharing the stories contained in these pages.

John Hannon
Sarasota, Florida
November 2016

FOREWORD

As the author of four bestselling business books on leadership, management, and employee engagement, I've been approached by several authors wanting me to write the Foreword for their book.

This is the first time I've ever said yes. In fact, I jumped at the chance.

That's because I read John's first book, *Engaged Management, Volume 1, Inspiring Your Team To Win* and found it to be one of the best management books I've read in the last decade. It was one of those "can't put it down" books that I didn't want to end. The stories captured me, the analogies enlightened me, and the strategies he gave have had a huge impact on me, both personally and professionally. When finished, I turned to my wife and said, *"I'm glad the title says this is Volume 1, cause it means he's gonna have to write a Volume 2!"*

Imagine my surprise and joy when John Hannon asked me to write the Foreword for this book.

Anyone who's ever been around him for more

than 5 minutes knows that John Hannon is a master at engaging others. In a world that's becoming less personal by the nano-second, John is able to personally connect with customers, clients, vendors, suppliers, associates and employees, and make each individual feel highly valued and tremendously important—because to him, they are. From there, he puts the entire focus on them as he listens to them with both ears to discover what makes them tick and what they're hoping to achieve. It sounds simple and perhaps common-place, but the exact opposite is true. Whether the person he is talking to wants to close a huge sale, attract better talent to their sales team or improve their golf game, John is all about helping leaders break barriers and achieve astounding results.

I've studied, researched, and written about employee engagement for the past twelve years. I've heard the collective groans of employers in all fields and industries lamenting that the existing talent pool is drying up and that loyalty is a thing of the past. Those who refuse to abandon the old-school "command and control" management strategies and tactics of yesteryear are crying the loudest as their best people are now bailing on them in droves. The winners in this brutal war for talent are those innovative thinkers who know how to connect with their people, prove to them that they're valued, and help them get from where they are to where they ultimately want, or need, to be.

I tell you this because if you're going to spend your valuable time reading a book with the words *engaged* and *management* in the title, there isn't anyone more qualified to write it than the author whose name is on the cover of this one. It will change the way you see yourself, your people, and your mission in life.

If you're looking for the go-to resource on finding, developing, managing, motivating, and keeping great salespeople, you're holding it in your hands. Dig into *Engaged Management, Volume 2, Maximizing Your Team's Sales Performance* and let the ideas and actionable techniques and strategies wash over you.

I assure you that if you release your preconceived notions about what used to work and let the master of engaging others guide you, you'll get to where you're going, help the people you lead get to where they're going, and you'll have a lot of fun along the way.

Eric Chester, Founder of the Center for Work Ethic Development and Author of *On Fire At Work: How Great Companies Ignite Passion in Their People Without Burning Them Out* and *Reviving Work Ethic: A Leader's Guide to Ending Entitlement and Restoring Pride in the Emerging Workforce*

INTRODUCTION

Every year, the day after our November broadcast event, we gather the Jim Doyle & Associates leadership team and set about the task of reviewing our company. It's a time-consuming exercise in which we dig deep into our operation to ensure that each individual's effort ties into our company priorities. At the same time, we check to make sure our work processes adhere to our posted fundamental beliefs. These beliefs guide our day-to-day interaction with our client partners.

Our planning session typically begins with a recap of the things we did right and the things we did wrong during the course of the year. As the new year begins, we will seek to amplify the things we did right and correct or, more likely, drop the wrong actions. We have to in order to get better— for you.

I'm proud to report that, as of this writing, the most recent year was yet another record year for our company. The fact that many of you are our loyal clients, partners, and supporters is not lost on me. Daily, we are thankful for your trust and confidence in what we do.

When the team has a good year, it's important that everyone gets to reflect on what was just accomplished. As a manager or leader, it's your responsibility to pump the breaks and encourage everyone to soak in the moment. After all, isn't that what winning is about? It's the elation resulting from the culmination of planning, hard work, and execution. It's the "we did it!"

Getting to the "we did it" is not easy. But, by reading and studying this second of a multi-volume book series, my hope is that you will gain clarity in selecting the most direct, and ultimately, the easiest path to success—however success is defined by you and your team(s).

At our company review meeting, it occurred to me that as a team we're better than we have ever been. But because we're hard-charging drivers, I know that we will one day move beyond that level of performance to new highs that we never thought possible.

The real opportunities, in any capacity of life, are the wins beyond the first win. The key to *maximizing your sales team's performance* starts with a vision that supports the idea of continued improvement for repetitive wins and a team that embraces the thought that right now we're better than we've ever been, but we aren't the best we're ever going to be.

CHAPTER 1

LEADING THE TEAM

When it comes to the growth of the company the leader is the limiter. -John Maxwell

TRUE LEADERS POSSESS A BUILD-A-BENCH VISION

At an NAB event in Las Vegas, a broadcasting group manager approached me and introduced one of his news directors. The news director quickly sized me up and said, "I know you." Not recognizing his name or face, I responded, "Where did our paths cross?"

"Our paths didn't cross," he replied. "I recognize you from your sales videos."

It's not uncommon to be recognized by unfamiliar faces of sales professionals or managers who interact with our teaching and training products. However, a news director identifying me after watching our videos is a first. So, of course, a deeper dig was in order.

As the conversation continued, I was impressed.

3

This news director had a career goal. He wanted to be a television station General Manager. While his news skills were impressive, he recognized that he was deficient in sales experience. He dedicated nights and weekends to viewing sales videos and reading sales books. He had set a goal and defined a path to get there. Do you think one day this news director's career dream will come true? I know it will.

Many years ago, long before joining Jim Doyle & Associates, I was recruited to meet with a broadcasting CEO for a GM job. During the meeting, the CEO stated, "In full disclosure, the opportunity we have is a news fix situation. I'm not so sure you have enough news background for this GM post." Surprised by the statement (did I mention *they* called *me*?), I said something rather weak like, "Well, from my experience, anything can be taught and learned." What I should have said was, "You were a radio CEO before becoming a TV CEO. How did you deal with not having TV experience in that transition?" Better yet, I should have wrapped myself around a news director's leg and made them teach me to better prepare for any such objection. I didn't get the job from the CEO seeking a GM news fixer, but ironically, within six months I was on the launch team of a national morning news show.

Why do I tell you these stories? Surely within

your organization there are hungry individuals with big career goals. If you want to transition from manager to leader, the biggest favor you could do for your company, and the industry in general, is to identify these future stars, cultivate their enthusiasm, and give them opportunities to grow toward and into their dream. Their growth is difficult without your guidance, so don't be hesitant to suggest corrections when they're headed down the wrong path. At the same time, when warranted, you need to brag about them to higher-ups to provide the all-important exposure that will keep them top of mind and in cue for the call up to the big leagues. This process is called building a bench, and leaders who master the process hold the key to many multiple years of repeat success within their marketplaces.

HELP YOUR TEAM FIND THEIR PASSION AND COMMITMENT

To reach the apex of television advertising sales success, one must have a passion for the business. Sales winners possess a commitment and energy for prospecting, developing, and completing sales opportunities. Unfortunately, this passion and commitment cannot be taught. However, as a sales manager and leader, you can groom and mentor select sellers to help them find their passion and increase their commitment.

The first step is to reinforce the value proposition of your products and services. Your AE's need to believe that there is an unlimited supply of prospects who need, want, and will benefit from your products and services. Support your argument with client testimonials and historical data showing growth trends and better-than-expected return on investment for key clients. Ever wonder why your digital sideband channel always has available inventory? It's because your sales team doesn't believe it has the power to benefit clients.

As the great UCLA basketball coach, John Wooden, said, "Failing to prepare is preparing to fail." Work with your stars to develop a road map to achieve win-win goals. Make sure their goals are in line with your department goals, which are in line with your station or cable outlet expectations. The goals should not be unrealistic but should possess a slight stretch factor to keep the seller focused.

Ask your AE's to present their accountable plan for consistently filling their sales funnels with prospects. Author and speaker, Stephan Shiffman, reminds us, "I need to prospect on a regular basis. That is the key to my sales plan." Not having enough business opportunities on deck to replace the prospective "yes's and no's" is a recipe for a sales slump—a slump that could easily be avoided with a bit of accountability and a new business call plan.

Lastly, be an exemplary example. Because you've been rewarded with a sales management title means you have, at some point in your career, enjoyed sales success. Lesser experienced sellers are watching you. They're adjusting and matching their own passion and commitment to your example. Lead by example. Engage your team. Help them understand what it feels like to win. Teach and train them, earn their respect, share the voice of your experience, and then get out of their way to let them do that which you have best conditioned them to do!

FOUR THINGS YOU MUST DO IN THE SECOND HALF OF THE YEAR

Every year at the same time on the calendar, July arrives. It marks the end of the first half and the beginning of the second half of the year. It's the opportunity to establish a clean slate, to right previous wrongs. This half-way reset is a time to learn from the first six months of the year by asking questions. Which mistakes did you learn from? What are you going to do differently? What seeds sprouted in the first half that you will now harvest? What changes, if any, are you going to incorporate to make you, and/or your team, better?

Check your calendar, circle July, and file these *four* things you must do in the second half of the year. Putting your best effort forward in executing these suggestions will help you end the year on an upswing.

1. Proper Management of Political Spending Expectations. Likely, you have more than once been on the receiving end of record level political advertising spending. In a word, each new political cycle sets "crazy" television advertising spending records—into the billions of dollars.

Two "P's" come out of this influx of cash: Profits and Pre-emptions. Television groups report record profits, thanks to 100% sellout levels at record rates. At the same time, television stations and cable outlets won't be able to hold all the placed money, as capacity has nowhere to go and commercials continue to get pre-empted, thanks to higher incoming rates. Many of the pre-empts will, unfortunately, be year-round loyal advertising clients.

Now is the time for a final double-check of your rate card. Are your columns set up to justify and maximize buyer risk-reward? You won't get this accomplished with mere $25 and $50 column jumps.

Make sure you have solid digital fallback plans for those local clients with nowhere to place their pre-empted commercials. Better yet, now is the time to have a conversation with those clients discussing the benefits of reaching their target via your digital offerings, instead of trying to compete on rate with the crowded, overpriced political announcements.

Think outside of traditional commercial offerings. If your master control operation has Miranda or Dekocast equipment, you're more than capable of offering other-than-traditional on-air commercial exposure via bugs, squeeze-backs, lower third messages, and sponsorships.

Lastly, be honest and patient with AE's during these heavy political advertising windows. Unless your office pays out on AE losses from a political pool, the AE's are losing money through no fault of their own. They'll need your help.

2. Bench Strength and Team Upgrades. Speaking of AE's—are you completely thrilled with your team or is there a weak link whom you have yet to help find a new career path?

Nearly every sales team carries along under-performers. When revenue is good, the mediocrity of these underperformers gets lost in the positive momentum of the team. Their shortfalls get overlooked because the team is exceeding budget. Did you ever stop to think how good your team could be or how much over budget your team could perform if the lackluster player was replaced with a sales go-getter?

Great broadcasting and cable sales managers realize that in order for their teams to perform at consistently high levels they need to do a regular staff pruning of the dead weight. The best time to upgrade the staff is when big money is pouring into your coffers. It's a mistake to wait until revenue dips to make a change.

Think for a second about the transition from a record revenue political year to a non-Olympic, non-political, odd year. The time for change is not in the middle of the revenue recovery fight. The additional team horsepower should be added before the end of a record revenue year, so that your team is running full-speed and ready to take on the challenges of an anticipated difficult selling environment.

3. Manage Up With An Operation Plan. It's a shame that the celebration of a successful year barely takes place before the discussion of the "off revenue" year begins to take place. During these transitions, you have no doubt picked up on the comments or tone from your corporate staff regarding their revenue concerns. Maybe your budget process becomes a bit more cumbersome than previous years. I have a tip to help you with your budget strain—have a plan. Yes, it's that simple. Your bosses report to shareholders or bankers, both of whom want to hear a plan on making up revenue in an off year. You have a chance to be the hero by managing up. Instead of waiting for the corporate, "Here's what we need your station to do next year" discussion, why not formulate an aggressive plan, specific to your operation, for pre-budget discussion with your corporate boss? In doing so you can help your boss formulate thoughts for the shareholders and/or bankers. You'll also stand out as a go-getter, and you may even get lucky if they adopt some of your suggestions and take them group-wide, enforcing your "wants" on other stations.

Your plan should begin with the standard SWOT (Strengths, Weaknesses, Opportunities, Threats) analysis and, because we're in a "for profit" business, all suggestions should have a revenue drive or goal.

Some example considerations are: staff purges and team upgrades; specific training implementations with expected revenue outcomes; client "whales" and hot category targets you will attack (for example, healthcare and attorneys); sales promotion initiatives you're pre-selling; a formal mega-performer new business and local direct bonus reward (don't forget the ROI on this bonus investment); expected or proven daypart/program ratings increases where you'll grow CPP and, in turn, revenue shares; adoption of non-traditional or digital sales programs and/or specialists; operational efficiency improvements.

4. Deposits. Deposits should be positive meetings of appreciation and relationship/trust building that are divided into two forms: client and employee.

These touches have to get scheduled into your calendar or they will never be done.

Client deposits from management during heavy political advertising are extremely beneficial. During these windows, the client is having trouble keeping their commercials on-air. When you or another manager reach out for an informal lunch, it gives you the opportunity to hand-hold while explaining the situation. But it's also a chance to inform the client of the favors and behind-the-scenes maneuvers you're making on their behalf. It's a pretty good bet that your competitors aren't making this move and, as a result, you will be positively remembered. It's especially important to be pleasantly top of mind with your key clients as you transition into a new year and you'll need them to maximize their budgets on your airwaves.

When scheduling these meetings, start with your current largest advertising clients, followed by the largest local market budgets, and then end with the clients who have the biggest budget growth potential.

One-on-one employee deposit meetings are as important, if not more important, than client deposit meetings. Take your stars out to lunch and let them know how much you appreciate them and their hard work, and how important they are to the success of the team. This is an opportunity to let your stars know how much their leadership is valued and how they'll be tested in the upcoming year. They'll enjoy the attention and the pat on the back. As your trust continues to grow, they won't want to disappoint, and ultimately, they'll become cheerleaders, pushing everyone else to the team goal.

A Culture Change Doesn't Happen Overnight

It seemed to be a longer than normal four-day road trip shadowing a few of our star Senior Marketing Consultants. These "observation" trips are necessary to make sure our training connects and that our partner stations are getting a return on their investment. A bonus during these trips is the time in between and after client presentations that I get to spend with sales teams and managers. These one-on-one breaks provide incredible insight into some of the nation's best television sales operations.

During one such sales observation trip, I was privileged to visit two high-performing, 50-plus-share, "boomer" stations. They're unrelated and in different markets, but other than that the stations are nearly identical in operation. I know what you're thinking: *If my station commanded a 50 share we could make a lot of money and be high-performing too.* Not always true. There are many dominant stations that, because of their less than desirable work environment, are falling dramatically short of their revenue potential.

Certainly, we can agree that high-rated stations do enjoy a bit of negotiation leverage. But rate is not the top priority in the big picture. The attitude and office culture will dictate an operation's long-term success.

The thing that struck me during my visit was that each staff, despite being #1 in their respective markets, acted like they were #3. The AE's were on offense, not defense. They dressed professionally, walked fast, spoke confidently and passionately, delivered customer-centric presentations, and wasted very little time, if any, making comparisons to the competition.

New business was still a priority no matter the seller's tenure. They held each of their peers accountable. Most pushed themselves harder and set higher goals than any manager would have expected. Lastly, they were not afraid to say "no," but did so professionally.

Can you imagine how much better your revenue results would be if you had a team like I described above?

When asking one of the sales managers how his team arrived at such sales success, he responded, "I don't know. I've been here 23 years and it has always been this way." The sales manager was not clueless. In fact, his answer gave me the opposite opinion. The success was so deeply ingrained for so many years that it had become self-fulfilling. Many at the station knew no alternative to winning, and individually they were not about to be the first to let their teammates down.

Please understand, teams don't wake up one morning and suddenly decide they're on the mountain top. Many years previous to the current staff, someone—a leader *not* a manager—created a vision, promoted buy-in, and championed a winning culture.

If you're unhappy with your environment's current culture, why can't you be the leader who steps forward and initiates the plan to build a foundation of positive momentum? I can't tell you the steps. An in-depth SWOT analysis of your team and market conditions will help determine your next move. But beware, establishing a team mindset takes time and will mentally test one's guts—your persistence, barometer of change, and leadership ability.

As a television sales manager you have a choice. You can continue with the status quo *or* you can make a decision to stop admiring great sales teams from afar and commit yourself to building a culture that your competitors envy.

INSIST THAT YOUR SELLERS LIVE UP TO THEIR TITLE

WARNING: You may be offended by what you are about to read.

When I was on your side of the desk and had to present unpleasant points to a group of sales managers or a sales team, I used to say, "If you find yourself asking, 'Is he talking about me?' guess what, it's a pretty good bet that I am."

I need to get something off my chest. My frustration is with TV sales managers who allow the sales team to negatively manage up. This isn't about managers who offer rate guidance or those who place general-to-general calls or maybe offer an occasional critique on a presentation or client letter. No, my reference is directed at TV sales managers who allow themselves to be a dumping ground for day-to-day sales tasks that should easily be turned back to AE's.

For example, on one market visit I sat in shock upon finding out that a sales manager had prepared *four* client presentations from start to finish (including the schedule and deliveries) for a single AE who either could not or would not do it themselves. This information didn't come to light until the client asked the AE, "Why are there no NFL games in this presentation?" The senior level, never-going-to-be-a-future-sales-star responded, "I don't know why NFL wasn't included. My manager did the schedule."

Or, how about the mid-market manager who spent half of her day calling and confirming client appointment times on behalf of AE's who were too busy with other projects to be bothered. This is the same manager who got in her car and drove to an agency after hours to hand deliver a forgotten invoice that an AE had promised to deliver earlier in the day.

Sound familiar?

What would possess a sales manager to do an AE's job for him/her? Some managers do this knowingly (think martyrs) and some do it unknowingly. From my experience, more than a few reasons come to mind:

- **A need to be liked.** What better way to be liked than to make life easy on the sales team?
- **Job security.** Some managers feel they need to be involved in every task possible. Sure, it may take a little work, but by doing so things get done that otherwise would not be completed.
- **Paranoia.** In the form of fear of losing their own job or fear of losing a person who may be perceived as a great seller.
- **Control.** (a) No one can do it better than me or (b) It's easier for me to do it because the AE can't do it or will screw it up.

There are a few pitfalls for sales managers who are guilty of being managed by the sales team. This type of manager is simply a manager, not a leader. As a result of being a bit of a pushover, the manager loses credibility with the sales team. Ask any AE and they will tell you that sales teams want *leaders.*

Everything tends to be completed last second or just beyond the deadline because there are only so many working hours in a day. For someone who cannot say "no," the long work days always end unfinished. And because deadlines are always pushed, the quality of work suffers and the AE's take no responsibility for the work since the managers controlled the process and the presentation.

Finally, the AE's never learn to work for themselves and the whole sales machine shuts down in the absence of the sales manager.

Careers can be negatively affected when managers don't hold AE's accountable. Because a manager has *not* taken the time to build a bench and didn't foster a system to mentor, groom and train sales team members to move to management, the sales manager is faced with limited promotion opportunities. After all, how could an AE be ready to assume a manager's chair if the manager has done all of his or her work?

Too many months, or in some cases years, of this style of operating creates burnout. What manager enjoys coming in early and staying late to complete projects and presentations, while sellers casually arrive late and leave early? Unless corrected, the manager is running on a never-ending treadmill, trying to catch up and never being able to fully stretch their wings to maximize time with the priorities or things that count.

Titles are on cards to distinguish roles within an organization. Do yourself a favor and place the performance of sales tasks squarely back on your sellers' shoulders and push them to live up to their title. Hold them accountable. Ultimately, if they cannot keep up with the job description, then maybe it's time for you to free them so they can find another title that is a closer match to their talents.

WANTEPRENEURS VS. ENTREPRENEURS

Often, I'm asked, "What is the #1 trait in successful salespeople?" In traveling the country and witnessing all kinds of sales styles, I'm convinced those individuals who possess a spirit of entrepreneurism are the most successful. These sales pros organize and work their account list as though it were their own business. They are hungry and motivated to push themselves to new revenue highs. These individuals do the things that average sellers won't do or aren't capable of doing.

I was reminded of this watching an episode of the TV show *Shark Tank*. It airs on ABC and CNBC and features *five* extremely successful, self-made multi-millionaires who listen to pitches from individuals seeking financial backers to help launch their business.

One of the show's hopefuls had invented a

cologne called "Money." The concept was interesting, but it was obvious the presenter lacked confidence in the product. The future business tycoon was seeking $150,000 for a 20% stake in his business. He stated, "In a $15-billion-a-year category I would consider us a success if we did a couple of million dollars in sales."

Billionaire ex-dotcom mogul and current owner of the Dallas Mavericks NBA team, Mark Cuban, immediately jumped in. "You stated this is a $15-billion-a-year category and you only want $2 million in sales? That statement tells me you lack drive and vision. An *entrepreneur* sets his sights high and wants all the money. A *wantepreneur* is satisfied with much less and is never able to drive the company to its full potential. You sir, are a wantepreneur and I do not want to partner with you."

Apparently, Mark's tone was consistent with the entire panel as no one offered an acceptable offer to partner in the business venture.

Is your sales staff comprised of entrepreneurs or wantepreneurs? My hope is that your staff make-up is predominantly entrepreneurs. If not, you likely lose sleep over team performance in categories like new business, local direct, station projects, and share reports. You probably get tired of repeating yourself and covering the same information multiple times. Sometimes you might experience a push/pull mentality, similar to trying to turn a barge, when it comes to motivating the team to adopt new initiatives or stretch for new revenue highs. Oh, how much easier life would be if your team was comprised of entrepreneurs.

You may be asking yourself, "Great John, I get it. But how can I move my team from being wantepreneurs to entrepreneurs?" Good question. It starts with you and the example you provide for a staff that is always watching your lead. Walk slow, lack a vision, avoid money-making priorities and sit in the office all day, and your staff will do the same. If you can honestly look in the mirror and state that you are "buttoned up" and you are an entrepreneur, then the staff change begins with tightened accountability and faster expectations.

I like to say, "As the pace around here quickens, AE's who could work for us *two* years ago can't necessarily work for us today." Let's face it, some sellers will never be entrepreneurs and will excel in mediocrity. You have to make a tough decision and have a plan for freeing the dead weight for bigger and better opportunities elsewhere. In the meantime, it's your responsibility to identify market entrepreneurs and make quick friends with them. It's a recruiting process that allows you to get to know them by spending multiple visits over coffee or lunch to see if they're a fit for the vision you have for the team. When, and if, the timing is right, both of you will know it.

Don't be afraid to use your own airwaves to advertise for sellers, whether you're looking to add to the staff or not. Doing so will keep the current team on their toes. You need to create a culture that states that no one is guaranteed a seat at our table. Perform and we will take care of and praise you. Everyone will understand the unstated alternative.

Lastly, patience is key when rebuilding a team of wantepreneurs into an entrepreneur machine. This will not happen overnight, but you can speed the process by quickly dealing with issues or individuals who slow your goal progress. Deep down, you know what you need to do. In this situation, the difference between a manager and a leader is that the manager adds fixing this problem to a "to do" list. The leader makes dealing with the issue or person a top priority.

DOES YOUR GENERAL MANAGER MAKE SALES A PRIORITY?

I was doing some management research for one of our Sales Manager's High Performance Boot Camps and stumbled across the NAB's "Guide To Careers In Television." I want to share with you a portion of a job description from the guide that got my attention. The description is that of a general manager:

"...They create a clear vision for the station and the blueprints for success that every staffer is expected to follow... The bottom line stops with the GM, who is charged with growing the station's profitability. Advertising revenue is crucial to a television station's financial security and, as a result, relationship-building with advertisers and potential advertisers is a significant area of the GM's responsibilities. The GM is heavily involved in the station's sales efforts and is generally expected to participate in sales presentations along with executive members of the sales staff. GMs find creative ways to profit and succeed despite obstacles..."

From my experience, the above description is not typical of general managers across the country. Most are superior at creating and executing a team vision. After all, they have to have displayed better than average leadership skills to qualify for the position. Unfortunately, many GMs fall short in their focus on sales. Why? Maybe they didn't come from sales and it's uncomfortable and embarrassing to admit what they don't know. Sometimes, GMs will claim that issues from other departments—news, promotions, etc.—fill their time and, at the end of the day, there's no room for GM sales time.

How about the GM who feels that he/she doesn't need to go on sales calls because their sales manager is so good? If the sales manager leaves and the GM doesn't have relationships with key accounts, then the revenue will surely be negatively impacted.

It's imperative for GMs to be willing and able to have high level sales conversations with large prospects and loyal key accounts. Market-revenue-leading media outlets possess leaders who aren't afraid to conduct general-to-general conversations. They understand that their office is "for profit" and the business of sales is their first priority.

If you're a media general manager reading this, I trust you're getting my point. However, if you're a sales manager wishing your GM was more active in building client relationships, then you need to keep reading because next I'll offer tips on "managing up" with your GM.

MANAGING UP WITH YOUR GENERAL MANAGER

Now that you understand the importance of general managers being visible in the sales process, I want to expand on what I meant by "priority." In today's competitive selling environment, GM's must, as a part of their weekly agenda, make themselves available for general-to-general client calls and key account discussions, or for any sizeable prospect who invests or is making the decision to invest their hard-earned advertising dollars in your medium.

Unfortunately, GMs who are truly committed to the sales effort seem to be in the minority. Today, I'm offering tips to sales managers who wish their manager was more active in building client relationships.

The first step is to ensure that your GM is aware of the culture and drive to revenue that you're creating in the sales department. Maybe your manager doesn't have a sales background and, as a result, stays away from your department to avoid embarrassment. The easiest way to educate without questioning knowledge is to make regular deposits.

Deposit Ask

- Make sure at the beginning of each year, quarter, etc., you provide your GM with your team's selling and projects calendar.
- Invite your manager to observe a sales meeting—once a month or at a time that's comfortable in their schedule.
- Slide the weekly sales meeting agenda under their door. Before doing so, write a few notes on the sheet like, "Team is really excited about Olympic prospects" or "Pacing +19% on college basketball revenue," etc.
- After each sales training meeting, make sure to provide your GM with a copy of the training handout and your notes. Consider emailing scanned copies.

Now that your manager is familiar with the "goings on" of your department, it's time to increase the "ask" to get them closer to making sales a priority. They'll do this by gaining confidence through building relationships.

<u>Relationship Ask</u>
- Invite them to host a sales training meeting that concentrates on how their career "voice of experience" can help your sellers achieve higher revenue returns.
- Each Friday, provide a list of names and phone numbers (not more than 2 or 3) of clients to whom you'd like the GM to leave an after-hours voice-mail message thanking them for their partnership. Please make sure to explain you're splitting the list with them and going through the same exercise.
- Ask her/him to shoot a video thanking national reps for their effort, and another video to use at the open of your station/outlet products DVD.
- Invite them to ride with an AE for a few hours to visit or maybe have lunch with key local direct clients. The GM's role on these visits is as an ambassador of your outlet. The intent is one of thanks and gratuity—basic relationship-building, not selling.

Note: If your manager is a chronic appointment canceller, do not tell the client when scheduling the lunch that the GM will be there. It's much easier to walk in with the GM as a surprise lunch guest than it is to make excuses when they're a no-show.

Assuming you've been able to "manage up" with deposits and relationships, your manager has established a bit of sales confidence and is naturally curious, maybe even excited, to participate in sales presentations. It's time for the full-on sales ask of your manager.

Sales Ask

- Request that a half-day each week be blocked on your GM's calendar to ride with AE's making presentations. It's important to clarify who will handle what portion of the sales presentation (AE or GM) so as not to confuse the prospect.

- Present a "whale" target list to your GM that he/she should attempt to contact and to make sales appointments. (Provide contact info, maybe a LinkedIn print and pic and an end date, or the calls won't happen.) These targets generally like to do business with big titles and appreciate when that preference is recognized. Typically, the closes are much larger than the average client. If your GM is skittish with this ask, remind her/him that you simply need them to get the appointment and show up with you. You'll handle the rest.

- Bring your GM on big-dollar or long-term

opportunities. These clients will appreciate hearing from the "top." Again, make sure to clarify presentation duties (who will handle what) with the GM and anyone else in attendance from your team.

My hope is that you needed none of my advice because your General Manager already makes sales a priority.

Please don't forget the importance of this message when it's your turn to sew on the GM stripe!

DON'T SKIP A STEP

Peak performance coach and author, Brian Cain, (www.briancain.com) tells a story of an "AH HA" moment that occurred on one of his high school visits. He was on his way to a football pep rally at Midland Lee High School in Texas, when he came upon a staircase and began skipping up the steps, taking them 2 or 3 at a time.

As Brian explains, one of the players yelled, "Stop... you can't go 2-3 steps at a time. Slow down." The player continued, "When you come to a staircase you must go only *one* step at a time to reinforce the belief that you *cannot* skip a step in the process and expect to make it to the top." What a great reminder that there are no shortcuts to success.

When was the last time you had a conversation

with your team, reinforcing the importance of honoring the sales process and taking one step at a time?

Step-skipping rears its ugly head when sellers get bored with the process. Sometimes AE's will change up the presentation because they've presented the same facts and figures a hundred times. So, they shake it up to entertain themselves. As a result, they forget where they are in the process and lose a bit of sales credibility. These AE's need to remember that the presentation is likely not boring to the client, as this is the first time they're seeing the show.

An abundance of confidence is another reason step-skipping occurs. Sellers will *assume* they know the answers to diagnosis questions and are unable to complete a thorough, "deep dig" or diagnosis. The outcome is a presentation that doesn't address the needs of the client, which translates to a "no sale."

Lastly, a lack of sales training contributes to step-skipping. As a television sales leader, it's your responsibility to provide formal sales training, complete with accountability and expectations. Many on your team "don't know what they don't know" and need guidance. By the way, depending upon your senior AE's to train junior AE's is a recipe for passing along bad habits. Sure, senior AE's provide a unique voice of experience and sales and mentor value, but they should not be relied upon as your sole training solution.

In short, skipping steps in the sales process prohibits opportunity. Money is left on the table, prospects are dismissed, time is wasted on non-prospects, presentations end without closing, referrals are lost—any number of negative outcomes can be expected.

YOU HAVE TO GET UP WITH THE ROOSTERS IF YOU WANT TO SOAR WITH THE EAGLES

During long weeks of various time zone travel it's easy to lose the morning routine of an early wake-up, then a workout, followed by a short period of reading or email, and then breakfast, all before a morning shower and the start of the workday. I'd been back home in Sarasota for *nine* days and was struggling to return to a positive morning ritual. Many times I'd opt to hit the snooze button and skip everything but the shower before heading to the office.

But this particular morning was different. I had an epiphany that provided all the leverage needed to drag my tired body out of bed.

It was still dark outside and was well before the crack of dawn when the alarm clock sounded with the shrill that we've all come to hate. While focusing my eyes on the ceiling, I considered *one* of *two* options: 1) reset the alarm for *ninety* minutes later and fall back into a blissful slumber, or 2) spring up off the mattress and start the day by increasing my heart rate and counting reps.

My mind picked #1, as it had so many of the last *nine* days that I'd been home. But nagging questions surfaced causing sleep to elude me.

- How many other people, at this very moment, are faced with this same decision?
- What drives the individuals who would never consider tapping the snooze button no matter how little sleep they got?
- How can I expect to win today if I choose the easy route, while others are willing to pay their dues and put in the work to create opportunities?

As sales leaders, isn't that often the same conversation we have with ourselves throughout the entirety of our days? "Do I go on the new business appointment with the AE or do I organize the stack of files on my desk?"

The answer is simple. What option delivers the biggest payoff and moves you closer to fulfilling priorities? In your gut, you know that going with the AE to see the client is the right decision. But if you consciously make the wrong decision, you can't be upset when the competition beats you. How much better would it be for you, and for those around you, if you cleared your mind of excuses and dedicated yourself to early, consistent, and dedicated performance?

You have to get up with the rooster if you want to soar with the eagles. On this particular morning I was reminded of that thought and, as a result, now welcome the early morning shrill of the alarm that I once despised.

INCREASING PERFORMANCE THROUGH THE POWER OF APPRECIATION

If you're a great leader, you understand the importance of employee celebrations. Holidays, birthdays, anniversaries, big sales, or any opportunity for team sharing, spotlighting, and recognition are common place in high-performing cultures. During a visit to our partner station WLEX, in Lexington, Kentucky, I was amazed at the employee excitement that General Manager Pat Dalbey was able to generate over a simple Thanksgiving luncheon. It was an opportunity for the entire station to break bread and enjoy one another's company, and the air was thick with enthusiasm.

That got me thinking. What do employees really want in the form of appreciation from employers? Sticking with the Thanksgiving theme, I discovered an Employee Appreciation Survey that was conducted by Harris Interactive on behalf of the talent and recruiting company, Glassdoor (www.glassdoor.com/press/employees). Here are the Thanksgiving perks, in rank order, that employees would most appreciate from employers:

1. Not be required to work the day before Thanksgiving, the day of Thanksgiving, and the day after Thanksgiving.
2. A cash bonus
3. A grocery store gift card
4. Pre-Thanksgiving meal at work
5. Not be required to work the days leading to Thanksgiving (Monday-Wednesday)
6. The ability to telecommute the days before Thanksgiving

There are really no surprises here. Days off and money trump all. How many of the above "extras" does your office provide?

The holidays are traditionally an expected opportunity for companies to express their appreciation through some form of additional gifting to employees. However, a few weeks of free "stuff" does not make up for a year filled with a shortfall of employee attention or appreciation.

According to the Harris survey, 53% of employees would stay longer if they felt more appreciation from their immediate supervisor. The upside is that 68% of employees felt their boss showed enough appreciation. The downside—you guessed it—32% need more appreciation. Where does your office (or maybe, more importantly, your management style) fall into this equation?

Here's what employees stated they value to feel appreciated:

1. Pay Raises 75%
2. Unexpected Treats & Rewards 46%
3. Involved In Making Decisions 40%
4. Career Development Opportunities 37%
5. Company-wide Recognition 35%
6. Opportunity To Do Interesting Work 34%
7. Variety In Their Work 32%
8. Telecommuting Options 26%
9. Company Sponsored Social Events 24%
10. Working With Colleagues & Departments 20%

Lastly, you want to increase your team's performance, minimize demands and threats, and look for opportunities to encourage. Why? Because only 37% of employees will work harder if they fear losing their job, 38% will work harder when the boss makes demands, and a staggering 81% will work harder when the boss shows appreciation. Apparently, appreciation trumps fear when it comes to motivating increased performance. That's proof that, as television sales managers, you can get more *wins* with sugar.

CHAPTER 2

COACHING TO WIN

If you don't demand your people maintain
high performances to remain on your team,
why should they be proud of the association?
-Coach Lou Holtz

EVERYONE ON THE TEAM TAKES GROUNDERS

The 2016 World Series featuring the Chicago Cubs and the Cleveland Indians was one for the ages. It took ten innings in the seventh game before the Cubs were declared World Champions, knocking off the Indians 8 to 7 on their home turf in Cleveland. It was indeed special to watch this baseball series, as it had been 108 years since the Cubs had previously held the title.

While watching the games, it occurred to me that *every* player on both teams had been dreaming and training likely for their entire lives for this very moment. I couldn't help but wonder if the teams would have been nearly as successful if only half of the players took batting practice or fielded grounders. After all, these players had made it to the big leagues. Why should they be bothered to do things that other, less talented players are expected to do?

The question is almost laughable.

In our business of television advertising sales, nearly every week I run into senior sellers who feel as though "they have arrived" and that somehow, because they have paid their dues, they are not obligated to prospect for new business. In other words, just like the above baseball reference, these sellers want to know why they should be bothered to do things that other, less talented sellers are expected to do?

In this context, the question *is not* so laughable.

If a senior seller is not writing new business on a regular basis and there are no repercussions in place, whose fault is that?

If the sales team lacks a new business culture, whose fault is that?

Lastly, if the sales team consistently falls short of their new business goal, whose fault is that?

Star television sales managers build their operations around the prospecting, cultivation, and sales of new business. Everyone on the team, from day one, understands it is THE #1 priority. It doesn't matter if you've been on the sales team 26 days, 26 weeks, 26 months or 26 years. The expectation is that *everyone* writes new business.

My friend and Gray Television station GSM, Ron Westrick, says it best, "*Everyone* on the team takes grounders."

Is the same true of your team?

Navigating The Agency And Client Relationship

In any business, one can find good and bad. The same is true of agencies. A good agency has the client's best interest at heart. They provide a diverse amount of services in order to ensure the client has success with their media strategy. A good agency is not afraid to include account executives on client calls, and they maintain positive and productive partnerships with media companies in the marketplace. On the flipside, a bad agency does none of the previously mentioned.

At some point in your career, someone at an agency has told you to "stay away from MY client!" In these instances, it was my practice to work quickly to establish a relationship with the business owner. It was my belief that the client is just as much mine as they are the agency's. The only reason an advertising agency would tell you to stay away from a client is because they possess a fear of loss. Likely, the client/agency relationship is on unstable ground, which is all-the-more reason to establish direct communication with the client. Many agencies will come and go. Just as a media contract renewal is not guaranteed for you, a client contract renewal is not guaranteed for the agency.

Recently, I was reading an advertising firm's blog and discovered a very disturbing quote. It's directed at agency clients and is a perfect example of why we need to maintain relationships with business decision makers, while continuing to educate agencies. It read:

"...When (the client) associates with the media in social settings, they are reducing the agency's effectiveness because now the media know they can bribe the client and they know the client's weakness. The rep also now knows he can circumvent the media buyer and go directly to the client. This is very bad for the client since they want the best deal and they want a professional firm to do the buying on their behalf. The agency's "power" has been lessened so the client loses. They no longer have the ability to negotiate with strength, because the rep knows if he can't get what he wants at the agency level, he can always go directly to the client."

Please advertisers! Let the agency do the job you hired them to do! Turn it ALL over to the agency, and let them direct you in what should be bought. Media reps work for the media, agencies work for the client."

Wow! Could there be a better example of fear of loss?

Thankfully, there are agency professionals who

"get it." Linda Kahn is one of the agency greats in the business. She's the CEO of The Ohlmann Group in Dayton, Ohio. She often expresses her belief in the importance of positive relationships with media companies. "We believe in tough negotiations, but we understand that we need to maintain the respect, and even the friendship, of our media partners." Linda continued, "We know the same partners from whom we buy are also the partners we want to turn to when our clients need assistance with things like promotions and value-added. We understand we need to play nice."

She also feels that an agency is an extension of the media outlet's sales staff. To quote Linda, "The more knowledge I have about a media company's products and services, the better I can help sell the station or channel."

Never forget that the retailer funds the whole process for *both* agencies and media companies. A successful client advertising campaign is best achieved through productive agency and media rep partnerships. Successful campaigns usually result in renewals and repeat business. Repeat business equals more commission for the agency and you!

A LESSON FROM A HOT DOG STAND OWNER

Have you heard the "Hot Dog Stand Parable" story? The source is anonymous but it's a great lesson about a man who didn't have any formal business training in accounting, engineering, law or medicine, so he did what most people do in those circumstances, he went into sales.

He opened a little stand on a street corner and yelled out "Get Your Hot Dogs!" His business took off immediately and grew with each passing day. So the man got a bigger griddle and hung a sign that read, "Hot Dogs." He did some advertising and his business boomed so much that he was able to put his oldest son through college.

The man's son came back with a degree in marketing and obviously knew everything there was to know about how to run a business. He told his dad there was a recession going on and that he had better change the way he did business—re-engineer, cut back.

The dad was scared. After all, his son knew it all, so the dad cut out his advertising, took down his "Hot Dogs" sign, reduced the size of his griddle, and even stopped yelling "Hot Dogs!"

He went home one day very dejected. His son asked, "What's the matter, Dad?" The dad said, "You're right, there is a recession going on out there and it's hit my business awful hard."

As you read that story, did any of your station or cable outlet clients come to mind? Worse yet, have you heard your AE's tell this story multiple times with an "insert business here" emphasis as the reason their billing is suffering? Maybe your sellers cry things like, "No one is buying because the economy is down." Or, "The election has people scared." Or, "Interest rates are rising and that makes advertisers nervous."

No doubt, there can be situations and legitimate reasons that business is off. But many times, business is off because of self-fulfilling prophecies. Business owners stop doing the things that enabled them to have sales success because they hear economic "what ifs." As a result, like the hot dog stand owner, business owners create their own unnecessary sales downturn—and your AE's accept it.

As a sales manager and leader, it's up to you to train your sellers to separate themselves from baseless negative "hype" conversations. Encourage educated testimonial and return on investment based discussions with clients. If your AE's do this, the client's fear of risk will be minimized and their positive momentum will continue to build through a continuation of their long-term marketing plans.

A Topic That Must Be On Your Training Agenda

Multiple times a week at our Jim Doyle & Associates headquarters in Sarasota, Florida, we receive questions or requests for sales help. The question most often asked is some form of, "How do I get to the client or decision maker?" Usually, this question is presented by newcomers to the business. However, there's a surprisingly high volume of senior sellers who ask the question as well.

So, what does that tell us? It tells us that we, as television sales managers and leaders, are not training enough on this topic. But I don't think this ends with just sales meeting training. The best way to reinforce and improve AE's who are suffering from difficulties with getting to a client or the decision maker is for them to observe a manager or veteran in action. Carve out some time in your schedule to mentor an AE and share your voice of experience with them. Ask them to suggest a prospect whom they're having trouble reaching and have them accompany you as you go through the steps of making contact. In short, teach them how to fish, again and again, until they have perfected the process.

Why is this important? Because most AE's give up way too early when attempting to call on new prospects, and that results in lost revenue! Many of today's young sellers will send an email and wait for a response—a response that never comes. Don't believe me? Below is an email exchange with a seller on this very topic. To protect the AE, the name has been changed. Could this be someone on your sales team?

Hi John,
As the new kid on the block, my account list is

small, so prospecting is the most important part of my daily activities. There are a couple of lawyers and doctors advertising in our market that seem to advertise on every station but ours. Due to the nature of their schedules, calling is a challenge and emailing hasn't been successful... any advice would be greatly appreciated. Thank you in advance.

Sharon, Account Executive

Sharon,

Thanks for reaching out. I'm going to suggest a few things that may help your effort to reach the decision maker, but first I'd like to address two points you mentioned in your question.

1) Your emails are not getting returned. Email is the absolute worst way to try to get an appointment with a prospect. Recently, in one of our partner markets, an auto dealer complained of how slow his computer was operating. Our Senior Vice President, Pat Norris, looked at the dealer's computer and found 9,974 unopened emails! Trust me, if you're cold-calling and hiding behind email to get an appointment, your email is not being read.

2) You mentioned they are advertising on competing stations in your market. That proves the prospects a) believe in advertising and b) will meet with AE's. So now is not the time to give up.

Your challenge is how to differentiate. How do

you intend to cut through the clutter of the nearly 150 vendors calling on a prospect? You have to stand out to make the client say, "This one is the one. I need to speak to this young lady because she can have a positive impact on my business." A few suggestions:

- Go to the business in person and ask for an appointment.
- Make nice with the gatekeeper, manager, spouse, etc.—someone who can serve as the bridge to the decision maker.
- Record a less than 2-minute video message directed at what you can do to help the prospect's business grow. Place it on a DVD or memory stick (clean, with no station logos) and handwrite with a sharpie, "Personal for 'Bob (Client Name)'" on the DVD or memory stick and on the outside of a plain (NOT station envelope). Hand-deliver it to the receptionist.
- Visit the business after, or before, business hours.
- Build what I call a "professional stalking" plan. Find out what clubs, organizations, boards, social hours, etc., the prospect attends and make it a point to casually bump into them.
- Lastly, it will take a few visits to build credibility before you ask for the order. You

have to make a deposit before asking for a withdrawal.

Please keep us updated on your sales success!

John

ELEVEN THINGS THAT MAKE THE DIFFERENCE

In the pages of our Jim Doyle & Associates *The Leaders Edge* weekly management newsletter, I spend a lot of time writing about the importance of local direct clients. Why? Because sellers can, for the most part, control local business. It becomes the foundation of any strong selling culture. However, we also understand that in any given market there are considerable dollars in agency business.

I first discovered one of my favorite "selling the agency" writings during a 2006 Account Executive hosted sales meeting. The piece, in its entirety, is below and is credited to Bob White, a 20+ year Senior Vice President at Ogilvy and Mather. The AE said Mr. White penned these thoughts in the 1980's, but the information is timeless.

How To Sell Me—Eleven Things That Make The Difference

I have been an Account Exec and a Sales Manager for almost 20 years at TV stations around the country. I switched sides about 5 years ago to the agency side and I have seen several hundred media salespeople from all media. Some stand out.

Most do not.

Over time, I have thought about what makes the difference—at least for me. Here are eleven things, in no particular order, that I believe begin to make a difference.

__1. Please come back.__ Good sales reps come back. The bad ones are "onefers." It is amazing how many reps are rude enough to take up your time once, but not nice enough to come back.

I know it's tough to get to see people. And I don't mean every week. But once you have broken the ice—I like you, I want to get to know you. I'm happy to hear about your progress, your product's success, even your kids.

__2. Tell me about your product.__ I don't know a thing about your product... nothing. Not the simplest details. I've got my own problems. I can't keep up. I'm drowning in my own responsibilities. I haven't got time to learn your business.

But, I don't want to embarrass myself, so I don't tell you I don't have the foggiest ideas about the simplest facts. I don't know how big you are. Who you are targeted against. Why people buy you or why I should. If I knew last year, I've already forgotten it—retell me—at least once a year.

__3. Give me a formal presentation.__ Put it on charts, or on your laptop. A deck or folder with expandable "pieces," commonly known as "one sheeters," are not a presentation, even if you go *through it. They, like a disc, are a leave-behind if I need further information. Folders sometimes become a book and they tell me too much. I end up chucking them out.*

Chart or presentation software means you will get to the facts faster, more simply. It forces you to stick to the basics and me to listen.

4. Know my people. *Who works on what? Where is your potential—by person? How can you work in a business if you don't know where everyone fits? Ask for an organization chart. Or force me to draw one.*

5. Don't miss anybody. *It's an old saw but true. Everyone counts: at the Agency, and at the Client.*

Everybody and nobody make decisions. It is a committee world. Cover the waterfront, make a pest of yourself. You'll annoy us, but we will do business with you.

6. Don't take the business for granted. *Change is constant. People, plans, dollars, timing. If you're not there to remind us why we wanted you in the first place, you won't be there to get the business when it happens.*

7. There is no right time to sell your product. *It's amazing how many reps show up at budget time. Frankly, that's too late. It's the idea that was implanted months ago that is written into the plan today.*

8. Give me an idea. *About how we use your (media)... that is your job. But don't stop there. Give me an idea about my product, or my advertising. Give me feedback; you are a consumer, tell me what you think. Tell me if I'm insulting you or selling you. Tell me how to improve.*

9. Make me feel you are in business with me. *Better yet, be in business with me.*

If you've been around the account group, the media group, the client's marketing group, you should know our business. Talk it to us; speak the language. Tell me about my competition. Tell me the street gossip. Tell me about the market. Tell me about my sales.

Invest time in me. I'll invest money in you.

10. It's still a people business. *Sure, we use computers; sure we are arbitrary about decisions based on them. But don't kid yourself, personal selling still gets the business.*

The fact is we bend over backwards to find a reason to put a friend—and I mean that in the business sense—on the list somehow.

If you're totally out on the economics you won't get in on salesmanship, but somewhere in my media mix is a question that won't be clean-cut. I'm going to be influenced by you. Help me, I'll help you.

11. If we have made a bad decision, let me know. *If you've been left out, or kicked out, let me* *know. Do it forcefully. If you're right, I'll know it.*

Maybe I'll change it. Maybe I won't. But, I will respect you. I'll remember you and I'll fight harder for you next time. I don't want to look silly twice.

OH CANADA!

A couple of years ago, Jim Doyle & Associates Senior Marketing Consultant, Don Fitzgibbons, (also an author, and the "Guru of Ads") and I were in Toronto for the annual Canadian TVB Sales Advisory Council event. Our television friends to the north had recently shown interest in our JDA sales teaching and training products, and this event provided us an opportunity to get to know some of Canada's industry players.

Some interesting observations resulted from the trip. There are *three* commercial groups and *one* quasi-government/private group in control of most of the country's television interests. The commercial groups also have telephone, mobile, cable, and internet divisions. Could this be a *ten-*year forward sneak-peak at the United States broadcasting and cable business?

At the event, it seemed women were just starting to make major inroads into the Canadian television management ranks. While there are always exceptions, we noted that female managers were predominantly first tier sales managers in Canada, while at the same time, media outlet sales staffs were comprised of about half men and half women. That was also once the picture in the United States. Thankfully, though, our American broadcasting and cable industries have made great strides in women earning management titles. However, there's still a bit of catching up to do in the television general manager and c-suite tiers.

From our observations, Canadian television needs are similar to your own. Managers are always on the hunt for good salespeople. They're expected to do more with less, especially in the larger multi-media companies where radio and newspaper convergence sales are a priority. Digital opportunities, while not as robust as in America, were slowly becoming expected in every presentation. Automated buying systems seemed to be more advanced in Canada, however, there was some concern that the ability to influence the outcome of a sale was removed in an automated purchasing environment.

Lastly, everyone with whom we met agreed about the importance of sales training as a foundation for a successful sales staff. The importance was reinforced with stories of whole staff turn-arounds resulting in record billing momentum. When I asked one Canadian manager what training they were currently using, his response was, "Oh, we had to trim expenses and didn't renew our training contract this year." It's funny, as I've heard that same answer in America. I'm always curious as to why an organization would view sales training as expendable. From my experience, removing sales training results in the loss of energy of what was once a fertile sales culture and ends with organizations trying to figure out why sales are off.

PUTTING A POSITIVE SPIN ON NEGATIVE WORDS

When walking the hallways of television stations and cable offices I often hear a lot of "TV talk"— conversations filled with words like *commitment, pitch,* and *contract.* In the office, that kind of talk is okay. However, when those kinds of words are used in presentations with clients, they create an unnecessary disadvantage.

Many of these words fall into what I like to call a "negative language" category. Because the words or phrases trigger fear or reminders to the client that they're being sold, they have the ability to portray your sellers in an unflattering light. You should train your sales team to eliminate these words and substitute them with positive replacements that, when used effectively, will help your account executives steer conversations to a sale.

I've listed some on the following pages for you. If you have some additions, please email me at john@jimdoyle.com

Eliminate	Replacement
Cost, Spend or Price	Investment
Advance Payment	Initial Investment
Monthly Payment	Monthly Investment
Commitment	Partnership
Contract	Agreement or Paperwork
Buy	Own (take ownership)
Selling	Helping them (you) market their (your) business
Signature	Approval, Authorization, Endorsement
Pitch	Presentation or Demonstration
Deal	Opportunity (for growth)
Spots	Commercial, Announcement, Invitation
First Right of Refusal	First Right of Acceptance
Decision-maker	Kahuna, Big Cheese, Who signs the checks?
Touching Base	Didn't have anything to say, wanted you to know I was thinking of you
Show you	Share with you
No	Yes
Can't	Can

Talk radio was playing in the background during my crosstown drive when the voices of unhappy callers caught my attention. Listeners were expressing their displeasure with different services they'd paid for and the jobs hadn't been completed, at least not to the purchasers' satisfaction.

But one caller's statement stood out from the rest and made quite an impression on me. The caller was detailing the botched job performed by an inept and supposedly experienced and certified plumber. The radio show host chided the caller for his selection of plumbers, and the caller, trying to save face, responded, "This plumber has commercials on TV so I thought they were reputable."

As a media sales manager, is there a box on your order sheets where your sellers have to check off that the advertiser is reputable? No, of course not. But public perception dictates that if someone is on TV they must belong in some elite business circle.

In 2016, *USA Today* reported the cost of an individual Super Bowl commercial surpassed *five* million dollars. A large percentage of the population doesn't understand the difference between a network rate and a local station rate. These folks are the ones watching the local car dealer commercial at half-time and telling the room that the dealer paid $5 million. Translation? Perception is not reality.

The public perceives that the businesses on TV have money and, as a result, are reputable. Bernie Madoff proved that a fat wallet doesn't automatically equate to premium service or a spotless reputation. Unfortunately, the thought persists. Worse yet, the thought persists with prospects and business owners.

How often do your AE's hear the objection that "TV advertising is too expensive"? As media professionals, we know it's simply not true. Your outlets provide varied price entry points, and digital products provide even more opportunity to maximize a return on investment when working with a client's budget.

Your sellers need to embrace the "big" perception of TV. AE/prospect conversations should look something like this, "Relative to other media, yes, we have massive viewing and digital audiences. We can put you and your services in front of thousands of potential customers. When properly executed, your sales will *dramatically* increase. You'll be surprised at how affordable our partnerships are, as even today, nothing can touch the return on investment of our services."

That kind of conversation will open the door to increased revenue. It should be a training priority to help your sellers capitalize on lost opportunities with business owners who don't know what they don't know.

THE REASON "ANY DAY" NEVER COMES FOR YOUR AE's

My suspicion is that less than a week has passed since an AE has excitedly assured you that a client was so impressed with a proposal that the deal would surely close any day. Let me guess at how the conversation might have gone. You (being the inquisitive manager that you are) ask, "What's the hold up? Why didn't the prospect give you a 'yes' today?" The AE, still excited, replies, "Oh, because the prospect has to get approval on the proposal from their boss first. But don't worry, she really liked the proposal. Getting approval shouldn't be a problem."

It's a pretty good bet that the supposed deal that would "surely close any day" is *not* going to happen. "Any day" never comes because your seller presented to a suspect, not a prospect. In other words, the fate of the sale rests in the hands of a gatekeeper or a non-decision maker.

AE's consistently get tricked into believing a pending sale is at hand, thanks to the cooperation and pleasant reception to a proposal from a non-decision maker. The decision maker empowers these individuals to "handle AE's" but they have no authority to deliver a yes or no.

Likely, you have trained your team on the importance of presenting *only* to those with decision-making authority. However, sometimes

AE's under call count pressure are so eager to get credit for the "up" that they don't fully qualify the person to whom they're presenting.

Spend some time with your newer sellers discussing ways to get to decision makers, as they tend to make more calls with *non-decision makers* or intermediaries than do more experienced sellers. They are not seasoned when it comes to professionally working their way around or working in conjunction with gatekeepers to get to the top of the decision-making ladder. Over time, the practice of presenting to intermediaries becomes a habit, which tends to *decrease* closing ratios while *increasing* frustration levels.

It's important for you to reinforce with your sales team that the best opportunity for sales success requires that *all* decision makers be present when asking for money. Doing so will increase the quality of "ups," and sales success will be a foregone conclusion.

THE ART OF TRIAL CLOSING FOR SALES SUCCESS

I was discussing with Jim Doyle the excitement expressed by a couple of our client AE's who have mastered the use of our *trial closing* suggestions to dramatically increase their commissions. In summary, right before the presentation's "ask," we teach sellers to casually begin a discussion of production and campaign deadlines. This usually causes the client to show their cards in one of two ways:

1. They'll stop the AE with some form of, "You're moving too fast" or "We aren't ready to commit."

   OR

2. They'll either ask if the deadlines can be changed or else agree to the proposed dates, at which time a seller knows the contract is closed before they even get to a formal ask.

Realizing there are many variations of the trial close, I decided to reach out to our team of Senior Marketing Consultants. These road warriors possess incredible marketing minds and are methodical sales presenters responsible for working alongside our television partner sales teams during client revenue initiatives. Collectively, our team of Senior Marketing Consultants conducts over 4,800+ advertising client appointments annually. You can find out more at www.teamdoyleconsultants.com

Here, a few of our SMC's have provided an explanation regarding their favorite trial closes:

Anne Fowler: During the presentation, I take a pulse check on the "three elements" portion. I'll say, "Does that make sense?" Sometimes they'll say "yes" but are shaking their head, indicating "no." That's my cue to give them another example or analogy that makes it relevant.

When I get to the close, I start with, "How do you feel about what we were able to put together for you?" Notice that the positioning is not how do you LIKE, but how do you FEEL. Buying advertising is an emotional purchase for many local businesses. Then I go into the timeline in an assumptive manner. If there are objections, they'll typically pop up during this portion. You overcome them one by one. I finish with, "The next step is crafting the creative vision. When is a good time to meet with production?"

Don Fitzgibbons: My favorite is a very simple statement with a bit of an assumptive tone. "Now, let's set up a meeting with production."

Jarrett McConnico: I sometimes open with a trial to set the tone for the call: "The strategy, tactics, and creative I've prepared are what I promised you when we met two weeks ago—all within the budget range we discussed. Is there anything that's changed since then or are we still on track to move forward?"

Some trials that I use throughout the entire presentation: "Are you with me? We good? Based on what you told me, this is _____, right?" (It's their idea.) "Your colleagues in your category have shared they have best results when_____. Do you agree? What would happen if business increased in the next 90 days by, say, 30%?"

Phil Bernstein: The closest thing I have to a "formal" trial close comes when I get to the timeline. I go through each piece of it: "Here's the way we see this coming together—if we can settle on the final script by February 9, the station can get it produced by the 21st. Amy will come out during the following week and play the commercial for everyone in your store. The campaign will start on March 1 in this scenario. After that, I would give it three solid months and then set up a meeting with Amy to go through the first round of results... Does this timetable work for you?"

Tom Conway: I like to say, "Does this make sense?" and "Are we good to move forward?" When I show the four screen TV/digital world slide, almost everyone says with a chuckle, "That's my living room." I respond, "But is it your media strategy? Probably not. Can I show you how to make that happen?"

WHEN AN EXPERIENCED AE SHOOTS LOW

Think of the players on your sales team for a moment. Are all of them maintaining rates? Do they maximize the value of the premium digital products and television programming that your operation provides? Is this true even of your newer hires?

Often, sales managers will reach out to us in frustration over this topic. Our last inquiry had a twist in that a new hire with radio sales experience was consistently shooting low and having trouble getting a satisfactory rate from prospective TV advertising clients.

The question: *"At our TV station, we have recently hired an ex-radio AE. The rep is very qualified and professional but is struggling with the radio to TV transition. They can close but they seem to have a low ceiling when it comes to clients and their budgets. Can you help?"*

Well, the good news is that a lot of the most successful TV sellers started in radio, so the odds are with you on this hire. Even better, from a management standpoint, this sales issue can be fixed. The bad news—the fix won't happen overnight because you're going to have to change habits.

What do I mean by changing habits? In this case, the TV station has hired an experienced rep, but the experience comes from a different medium. This individual has likely been conditioned that a radio audience reaches X *hundreds* and, as a result, each commercial is worth X dollars. The seller likely developed a comfort in presenting to clients who carried X budget. All of the "X's" a rep has worked with for years are likely much smaller than the X expectations they will encounter in the world of television advertising sales.

When hiring a rep away from a medium that sells

their inventory cheaper, and that typically delivers a smaller audience, the key is your communication to them regarding audience differences and their value.

Below are a few bullets to consider for discussion in helping your future sales star stop shooting low and start hitting the revenue bullseye:

- The best results from television advertising are achieved by owning something, e.g., programming, daypart, day, etc. Maximum results are not achieved by selling commercials in broad rotation.
- Generally, television advertising far out-delivers other media in audience delivery. TV is a media of multiple thousands of viewers vs. the hundreds consuming competing media. As a result, a rep who's transitioning needs to understand the rate expectations.
- Some reps will possess call reluctance, thanks to their lack of experience in asking for the large amounts of money that it will take to invest in your medium. Help them understand that the amount of prep time and the ask effort is exactly the same regardless of whether the ask is $1K or $10K.
- Experienced reps feel they know how to read

a client and will sometimes come to budget conclusions without having the important "money" conversation. Train AE's to have a professional discussion about the prospect's entire budget. Confidence levels change and ask amounts go up when a sales star understands they're competing for a share of $100K vs. their perception of a $25K max budget.

- You have to be diligent in your observation and guidance of the transitioning rep's prospect call list, proposal writing, and rate integrity. If they continue to shoot low, you need to step in and quickly correct their effort before it becomes a bad habit. For repeat offenders, feel free to give them an absolute minimum rate for every show. But, don't be surprised in the beginning when they sell every commercial at the absolute minimum. For a while, your minimum could be their highest ever rate. It will take time to transition. This observation, and guidance from you, is at least a 90- to 180-day window.

- If there is no belief in a product, it won't get sold. Don't assume an experienced seller knows everything. For all you know, they've been selling against your medium, station or cable outlet for years. They may not understand the value of the product(s) they will now be presenting to prospects. Take some time to separate perception from reality and school the new team member on true audience delivery, rate integrity, inventory management, and their comparisons to their previous medium.

GET WITH ME AFTER THE HOLIDAYS

It happens every year as the calendar approaches the holidays. I call it the "end of year holiday sales *delay.*" It's when your sellers go for the presentation close and the client responds, "Get with me after the holidays." I hated that response as an AE. Why? Because it seemed like a good excuse, but accepting it didn't help my commission check. In reality, I didn't know how to respond to that objection.

The key to revenue success for your AE's during the holiday season will hinge on their ability to talk through the objection to determine if the response is legitimate or simply a put-off.

Many times, a prospect is under holiday work *and* stress at home. Putting off a seller's "ask" stops one more commitment from landing on their plate. In these instances, when a client says, "Get with me after the holidays," your sales stars should counter professionally with a version of, "Can I ask what will change between now and after the holidays?" If the answer is a borderline "nothing," then your seller should attempt the close again, "If nothing will change, why don't we go ahead and take care of this now to free up your post-holiday time for more pressing issues?"

In addition, anything your AE can incorporate into the presentation to promote a sense of turnkey and streamlining will ease the "lack of time" anxiety for the client.

Sometimes, the objection is presented when the prospect has no intention of ever buying from your AE. That's OK. As humans, we generally don't want to disappoint and will, at times, stall a "no" with a delay statement. A seller's job in this case is to work the potential client into a "yes" or a "no." One can accomplish this by asking, "Mr. Client, often I hear that response when someone may be uncomfortable telling me 'no.' Do you feel there's a pressing reason to wait or did you want to tell me 'no?'" If the client responds that they mean "no," your AE's should ask, "Is that a 'no' for today or a 'no' for forever?"

Why am I promoting such a hard push for an answer? Because if the prospect has no revenue potential, then there's no reason to waste time with the client before *or* after the holidays. A legitimate "no" provides the confidence to move on to a more qualified opportunity after crossing the client's name off the prospect list.

Here's a bonus lesson for your team. Teach them to ask for a referral after a prospect has said "no" to a proposal. Many of these clients feel obligated to help after rejecting your seller's "ask."

RECOVERING FROM ADVERSITY

"We got beat. So, we're going to move on quickly… We've identified things that have to get better and we will, because that's what we do." These were the words of The Ohio State University head football coach Urban Meyer in a press conference immediately following the Buckeyes 31-0 loss to the Clemson Tigers in the Fiesta Bowl, the first round of the 2016 College Football National Championship Playoff.

In his 16 years as a head coach, never before had one of Urban Meyer's teams finished a game with a big goose egg—a zero.

In the darkness of adversity, real leaders establish themselves by discarding excuses, taking ownership of the moment, and putting the misstep behind them.

Coach Meyer did just that with his next statement, "Ohio State is *not* used to this. *I'm not* used to this and *we will not* get used to this. This is not going to happen again."

The message was delivered in such a deliberate tone and pace that Buckeye fans, and even non-fans, knew that under Urban Meyer's leadership, Ohio State would one day soon be back in the playoff picture and the outcome would be different.

How do you handle the situation when your team takes a loss? Maybe your team didn't keep pace with the market on the last revenue audit. Did you call a sales meeting to yell and scream, point fingers, maybe place blame? Or, did you take the hit, holding yourself accountable before detailing the work that everyone in the room was going to have to put in to rectify the situation?

The direction you take and the style in which you convey your concerns are directly related to the ability to reverse your negative fortunes.

Like Urban Meyer, the best leaders understand this.

CHAPTER 3

MANAGING FOR MAXIMUM PERFORMANCE

The ultimate test of management is performance. -Peter Drucker

WHEN YOU WANT IT MORE THAN THEY DO IT'S TIME TO SAY GOODBYE

Why do we, as professional media managers, allow the lackluster peddlers to occupy a seat on our sales bench? Be honest with yourself. Right now, on your sales staff there's one, or maybe a couple, AE's who consistently fall short of your sales expectations. Why are they allowed to remain on your team?

My bet is that less than desirable sellers occasionally sit in your sales pit longer than they should because you are human. In being human, you cheerlead the underdog when you note that their personal "sacrifice" is sincere. Maybe you can't justify firing someone who, by all appearances, is giving it their all. You convince yourself that some sales shadowing, more instructional tape viewing or the passing of time will move this person from sales loser to sales winner. Before you know it, this individual—your personal sales "project" who has just stolen nine months of your management time away from the rest of the sales team—is sitting across from you in yet another performance meeting, while you contemplate probation or firing.

At some point during this uphill climb, the account executive has grown tired of the fight and the lack of progress. They don't like having a target on their back. Their enthusiasm slows, and internally they begin to question themselves on whether this is the career for them. They begin to want "it" (defined as sales success, a broadcasting career, etc.) less. Very quickly, you begin to sense you want "it" more for them than they do for themselves. When this epiphany strikes, it's time for you to act upon something you should have done sooner—cut your losses and terminate the sales underperformer. I guarantee that both of you will feel better after the dust has settled and the ex-media rep is driving away from your office for the last time.

THERE'S MORE THAN ONE MANAGEMENT STYLE TO GET IMPROVED REVENUE PERFORMANCE

When entering a media outlet, it's easy to gather a quick sense of the attitude and morale of the staff. Typically, "it" is in the air. Very simply, I observe the warm or cold welcome of the receptionist and reception area, employee walking pace, the facial expressions, the staff awards and pictures—or lack thereof. In addition, my ears tune into far-down-the-hallway conversations, listening for enunciation, excitement, and laughter—all of which shows commitment. The combination of these assessments takes barely thirty seconds, but the observation is telling.

One would think that staffs suffering from low morale would not be able to perform. But that thinking isn't true, at least when considering short-term performance.

I recall a conversation with a relatively "new to the market" general manager who was quick to answer my questions as though he had no worries. My thirty-second assessment of his organization was that morale was the pits. The employees were walking around like they were headed to the salt mines. Yelling and screaming were on the daily agenda, and yet, surprisingly, the sales team was making budget.

Knowing that some of the sellers were seeking opportunity elsewhere, I asked the GM this question, "What happens if you lose the big sales biller or one of your managers? Do you have a bench?"

Without hesitation, the GM responded, "I don't care. There's a line of people wanting to work here.

Someone leaves, that's on them!" The troubling thing is, I know this manager meant and believed what he was saying. In his mind, salespeople are just a number; they're disposable.

Remember, I said the team was making budget. They did so for the next quarter, but then spent the better part of *five* consecutive quarters trying to dig out of a budget shortfall. The confident GM wasn't so confident anymore.

Apparently, perceived "good for business" threats and yelling and screaming are not long-term plans for prosperous revenue production. Worse yet, when word gets out about media outlets with this type of environment, lesser qualified employees will knock on the door and the staff talent pool will take a hit through multiple turnovers.

From my experience, there's more than one management style to get improved revenue performance. However, threatening, yelling, and screaming should not be your first choice, as it's a short-term fix that creates long-term problems.

A TWIST ON MEASURING NEW BUSINESS

Are you happy with your sales team's new business performance? Do they consistently fall short *or* over-deliver on your new business expectations? Are you confident that your sellers are capable of delivering the volume of new business needed to grow new business revenue in an off year?

New business sales goals, whether individual or team, are consistent with other goals in that effective managers create a plan of achievement. The plan is a road map to keep everyone focused on the task at hand. Likely, your road map includes a certain number of new business calls per week or month, a minimum monthly expectation of closed new business revenue, and maybe measurable expertise in prospecting competing media for new revenue.

However, there's a little known metric that most managers overlook when building their team's new business plan: the number of times an account executive calls on a *single* prospect. In Jack Canfield's book, *The Success Principles*, marketing specialist Herbert True of Notre Dame University details some very revealing sales call statistics (www.thesuccessprinciples.com). He reported this about salespeople and their prospecting efforts:

- 44% quit after the 1st call
- 24% quit after the 2nd call
- 14% quit after the 3rd call
- 12% quit after the 4th call

In summary, 94% of salespeople quit calling on a prospect after the 4th call, but... 60% of all sales are made after the 4th call. That means that 60% of prospective buyers are passed over by 94% of all salespeople!

Teach your future sales stars to commit to at

least *five* calls on a qualified decision maker. Statistics prove that professional persistence will pay off by delivering more new business revenue!

"C" MANAGERS CAN'T LEAD "A" SELLERS, BUT "A" SELLERS WILL LEAD "C" MANAGERS

"How can you expect your sales team to be their best if you aren't at your best?" It was a question I asked of a sales manager who was expressing frustration at the lack of performance from her sales team. She looked at me as though the question offended her. She had previously admitted some signs of personal burnout—that some of her passion for the industry had faded. She even questioned if she was still good enough to continue leading the team. The account executives didn't seem to respect her authority anymore and her attempts at accountability were ignored. It was as if the sellers were managing her... and she was right!

"C" managers can't lead "A" sellers, but "A" sellers will lead "C" managers. In the not-so-distant past, this manager was a winner—an "A" manager with the best group of sellers in the market. Personal issues spilling over into her work life and stress from a station sale were blows from which she'd had difficulty recovering. Somewhere along the line she'd lost control and the respect of the herd.

"Will I ever be able to recover from this setback?" she asked me. Predicting the future is not one of my specialties. However, I did explain to her that if she was sincere in her desire to be the best in the market again, she would first need to have a difficult conversation with her staff. This conversation would mark a new beginning in an effort to right the wrongs and capitalize on the opportunity for everyone to learn from the experience.

A few months later I saw my sales manager friend. Something was a bit different. She had a pep in her step and was walking fast, as many determined individuals are known to do. There were smiles in the sales pit and a lighter, not so intense feel in the air.

We got around to the topic of the team conversation. She explained how, for the meeting, she wrote down everything she wanted to address. This allowed her to keep her emotions in check and stay focused on the topic. Then, she started the team discussion with an apology, taking full responsibility for letting them down as a manager and a leader.

She said the turning point of the meeting was admitting she was human and capable of making mistakes. Many of the sellers apologized back and admitted their own mistakes. All agreed it was a new day and it would take the commitment of everyone on the team if they were to return to market leading revenue shares.

My sales manager friend smiled as she summarized the strained relationships and the ups and downs of the back half of the past year: "It's interesting how that negative experience has made us closer. The competitive fun has returned to our office."

CONVERTING OLD CLIENTS INTO NEW CLIENTS

How many clients used to invest in your television station or cable outlet but, for whatever reason, stopped and have since dropped off your staff's client list? To determine this "churn," it might be wise to have your traffic manager print a client tracking report. You might be surprised to find out how many advertisers fall into this forgotten customer scenario.

Once you have your list, the question is how to use it. I have two suggestions: 1) give the list to junior AE's and let them work it to see which of the clients are legitimate prospects or 2) create a bit of staff energy by hosting a contest with big prizes to reward those who close the most money (before an established deadline). Regardless of how you roll out the list, you'll need to have a plan for securing the return of these clients.

Many years ago, Adelphia Media Services waged a sales campaign called, **"Our Viewers Miss You!"** Their plan to sales success was broken into *four* steps:

1. **Identify:** Churned advertisers were identified in their traffic and billing information systems.

2. **Qualify:** These advertisers were compiled into a prospect list that was cross-referenced for bad debt and seasonal advertisers.
3. **Market:** Former advertisers received an "Our Viewers Miss You!" postcard offering these past customers a bonus airtime incentive for each $1,000 in purchased advertising.
4. **Sell:** Three days after mailing the postcards the Adelphia AE's followed up on these clients to set appointments. Prizes were awarded to the AE's who delivered the most revenue.

After one month, Adelphia claimed to have closed $310,000 with these "missed" customers.

Do You Have A Sales Business Plan?

While cleaning out some old files, I stumbled upon multiple sales business plans and revenue road maps that station sales managers and I had created over the years at my various career stops.

One of the business plans stuck out as halfway decent. It was from Dayton, Ohio, where the team consistently generated positive momentum that resulted in a pretty good run for the stand-alone WB, and later, a CW affiliate.

In retrospect, it seems our second and third place market revenue share peaks took a back seat celebration to our numerous "pole" positions in the national ratings race.

I guess we assumed the revenue growth would

continue to be there. We adjusted the sales business plan annually and executed it by the book. A funny thing happens when you confidently put out a detailed revenue plan and stick to it. More often than not, it works. Here's the verbatim plan:

A Television Station Sales Business Plan

Overview:

We commit to making winners out of our mixed staff of experienced and inexperienced sellers through the cornerstones of training, accountability, and recognition. Key to our success is "differentiation" among our television competitors first, and all advertising businesses second. Lastly, we will focus our concentration on three station goals:

1. Ask for copious amounts of money in an effort to surpass budget and maximize rate and share.
2. Build sales professionals and leaders.
3. Continue to set the sales operation pace for our corporate sister stations.

Sales Business Plan Components:

1. **Increase individual program rates and market revenue share**
   a. Fill inventory with the highest rate possible without negatively impacting business share,

i.e., packaging The Daily Buzz (morning news); sell the program not rotation; sell the "sizzle."

b. Tight tracking of CMR and historical spending to ensure opportunity in every market buy and ownership of key accounts.

c. Seek revenue outside of TV advertisers—specific digital help, print, music?

d. Face-to-face calls on political agencies.

e. Teach sports presentation skills.

2. Build premium sales staff and top market sales professionals

a. Prune, do not carry, dead-weight—AE's who could work for us three years ago but may not be able to do so today.

b. Training—consistent and ongoing. Develop AE leaders.

c. Coaching through listening and encouraging individual decision-making.

d. Recruiting—build a bench for unexpected needs.

3. New business and local direct business plan

a. New business solves all problems.

b. Concentrate training and expectations on building a salary upon a local direct foundation.

c. AE's get vertical in specific client categories.

d. Always propose *thirteen* weeks or better.

4. Build sales promotions
   a. Align promotions with staff survey priority results.
   b. Drop high-effort, low-return promotions.
   c. Concentrate sales effort on client cash participation instead of incremental.
   d. Continue assignment of AE "specialists" for Tier 1 and larger Tier 2 sales promotions.

NOT EQUAL GIVING, BUT EQUAL SACRIFICES

During Easter Mass I had trouble concentrating. It wasn't because of the beautiful music or pastel church decorations. Instead, it was a sign at the church entry that occupied my thoughts. The sign read, "Not Equal Giving, But Equal Sacrifices." The message was posted to encourage annual tithing, but for some reason, to me it held an alternative meaning to filling the collection plate.

"Not Equal Giving, But Equal Sacrifices." Let that sink in for a moment. How does that apply to your sales staff? Every staff has a few star sellers, an up-and-comer, one or two steady order takers, and at least one subpar performer with a foot out the door.

From my experience, the inconsistent or low-performing sellers are givers, but not in the positive sense. They view their position as more of a job than a career. They "give" the minimum time and effort it takes to keep you, the manager, off their backs.

Because their view is so short-sighted, they have difficulty believing they could perform consistently at a high level of selling. To be great would require something more than they're willing to commit to because in their eyes this is only a job.

Your stars view their profession as a career. They're committed to success and to that end will *sacrifice* and hold themselves accountable to the highest level of selling. They take pride in pushing themselves beyond monthly budgets. They "sacrifice" their time for longer work hours, their radio listening drive home becomes audio learning time, they study to become better and, as a result, new sales ceilings are easily discarded for bigger goals.

As a professional media manager, your job is to push each team member to new levels of achievement. You need to help them realize new sales highs that they previously never thought possible. Don't build a team that simply "gives" or goes through the motions to get past another appointment or day. True, a sales team that is giving will occasionally make budget. However, star media managers understand that sustained peak performance from a sales team is only achieved through hard work and *sacrifice*.

Charlie Finley, a sports marketing legend who once owned the Oakland A's baseball team, put it best, "Sweat plus *sacrifice* equals success."

THE SALE IS NOT COMPLETE UNTIL THE MONEY IS COLLECTED

The process of collections is a necessary priority and one that often falls to the bottom of the list, until an AE's commission is threatened. Could your sellers use some coaching in this process? Here are some steps to cover with your sales stars that may make them more comfortable in dealing with collections, which could help minimize your write-offs.

The first thing your sales team needs to understand is that clients who are behind in paying your office are likely behind in payments to other vendors. As a result, speed in contacting the client is important. You want to be first in the line of collections—before competitors start circling for checks. Waiting 90 days is too late. Condition your sellers to make a casual collection mention with their clients somewhere between the 45- and 60-day marks. The question should not be accusatory; it should instead be almost apologetic as in, "Mr. Advertiser, I noticed we didn't receive a payment on your November invoice. We had a hiccup in our statement mailing and I wanted to make sure you received yours." Encourage sellers to deliver another statement in person (and get the check while they're standing there). If in-person isn't available, then email the statement to the client with a return receipt to confirm the client has read the email.

Some clients don't understand that AE's can lose commission on advertising that goes unpaid. Explain to your team that as they establish personal relationships with a new client it's okay to reveal how compensation works inside the media company. It isn't necessary to reveal how much money they make or percentages, but simply how the process of getting paid works. Over time, if your sales star has built a personal relationship with a client, this information could be the difference between your office getting paid first or not at all when all vendors are lined up to collect.

If a client isn't returning calls, that's a major red flag that it's time to amplify the collection effort. Teach your AE's to collect information like client mobile phone numbers, fax numbers, personal emails, etc., early in the sales process. These forms of contact will need to be used when someone continues to hide from your seller's attempts to track them down.

Never accept the "check is in the mail" comment. Instead, your sales pros should offer to drive over and get the check, establish a payment plan, take partial payment, accept cash (get a signed receipt so there's no room for dispute on the amount brought to the office) or accept a credit card charge for payment.

The last tip: when it comes to concerts, shows or events, never deviate from the cash-in-advance rule. Once these performers leave town, your folks stand a slim chance at best of collecting any outstanding balances.

WHAT IS THE MAGIC NUMBER OF REPS FOR YOUR TEAM?

Every April, I have the pleasure of attending the National Association of Broadcasters show in Las Vegas. When taking this trip there's never time for gambling and rarely, if ever, do I even see the convention floor. Instead, this is an opportunity to sit one-on-one with some of the smartest television industry leaders in the country and get their impression(s) on the challenges and growth opportunities within the business. In addition, and probably most important for our company, is that this is a chance to have candid exchanges to ensure that our teaching and training fulfills client needs, that our services deliver a solid return on investment, and that our partnership, in the eyes of each group leader, is still relevant.

Many times I've said to managers, "If you're going to ask the question, be big enough to accept the honest answer, no matter how painful." I remind myself of that statement with each C-suite sit-down. Thankfully, the painful answers are typically few in number. The point is, in all relationships in work and life, it's communication and understanding and fulfilling needs that are the keys to relationship growth. That's why it's so important to take the time to have honest conversations about needs, wants, desires, and goals.

During the one-on-one meetings in the last few years, the theme of team head count seems to be a larger part of the discussion. Specifically, adding more "feet on the streets." I'm in full agreement that stations and cable outlets do not employ enough sellers.

Borrell Associates (www.borrellassociates.com) has calculated there are 80,826 US media reps knocking on advertisers' doors. By the way, the fastest growing segment of these reps are internet pure plays. There is entirely too much competition in today's selling environment to think that the same number of AE's who comprised your team *ten* years ago is adequate for today.

I consistently ask television sales managers, "How many reps do you have on the street from a single office?" Depending on the market, the answer is usually around 6 or 7. Then I ask, "What is the magic number of reps for your team?" Over 90% of the time the answer is, "One more..." Since the early 90's, the answer has been... "One more." For years, managers all over the country have been walking around trying to locate this elusive "one more" rep! This is outdated thinking. If you have 6 reps, the magic number should be north of 10 reps!

Going from 6 sales reps to 10 or more will not

happen overnight, nor will it happen without a roadmap. The plan to get there has to come from you. If it were easy, everyone would do it. But they don't, and the ones who don't will slug along, making budget from time to time, but will never really push the revenue budget to record levels. However, the managers who do possess a vision for growing the team and who commit to being the biggest sales team in the marketplace are the revenue leaders who consistently collect big bonus checks every time the audit ships. Which kind of sales manager are you?

At one of our Las Vegas NAB meetings, the COO of a broadcast company said, "One of my biggest jobs is to recognize obstacles for our sellers." I love that statement and can only imagine how productive the sales environments are for the managers who come to this COO with a revenue plan.

Don't Be A "Congratulations, But..." Manager

Executive coach Marshall Goldsmith tells the story of a young boy bringing his report card home to his father. The boy was hesitant to hand over the report card, fearing his father would be upset. Upon opening the card, the father observed 5 A's and 1 B. The dad hugged his son and congratulated him on the A's. The son said, "Father, aren't you going to yell at me for the B?" The father responded, "Why would I do that? You worked hard to get the 5 A's."

Do you celebrate when your AE's come through with a nice order? By "nice" I mean a contract that has a high dollar value or one that took perseverance or considerable effort to finally close. How do you convey *verbal* congratulations for the effort? Note: there's an assumption here that you do recognize that this moment calls for congratulations. Do you?

In my travels, I often hear managers celebrate sales victories. But many times, in an attempt to make a congratulatory deposit, managers don't know where the celebration ends and the insult begins. Retrospectively, I guess I was guilty of this more than once during my sales management career.

Here's what I mean—and I hope you don't recognize any of these scenarios: The sales manager who tells the team, "Congratulations. We made the 1st quarter budget. But... we aren't even close to our Olympic sales goal." Or, how about the manager who throws a compliment to an AE who just set a personal new business record, only to follow the compliment with, "But... you fell short of your total budget."

Over time, when managers practice this "Congratulations, but..." style of communication, sellers begin to wait for the other shoe to drop. AE's don't get a chance to bask in the glory of a victory because their leader can't help but state the obvious shortfall after a half-attempt at a congratulations.

But all is not lost. If you recognize that you're a "Congratulations, but..." manager, you still have time to change your bad habit. Simply condition yourself to have *two* discussions. Address the good and the bad independent of each other in two separate conversations.

ACCOUNT EXECUTIVES HAVE NEEDS

One of the most enjoyable things about my job is the opportunity to observe the myriad of television and digital sales operations across the nation. I'm always impressed with sales teams that seem to display no revenue ceiling, and as a result, consistently outperform the industry.

From my observation, there is one consistency among these high-performing sales machines—an incredible manager who understands the things AE's need in order to deliver optimum results. Are you curious as to what those AE *needs* are? I was too. So I pulled out my phone and videoed AE's explaining what they need from their managers. The answers at each stop were very telling:

"I need a manager to have a pulse on what's happening in the market. Make time to sit down with me for an update."

"As I continue to mature in the business and prove my worth, I need some flexibility, not micromanagement."

"Know my personality and motivators, and understand that I am different from the rest of the staff."

"Go on sales calls with me and help me close business. Make my clients feel special."

"Give me motivation, guidance, and suggestions for what may have worked in the past in a similar situation."

"Be a good listener before offering input."

"Mentor me, help me achieve my career goals. Train me to be the next manager."

"Surprise me by doing something random for one of my clients that was unexpected."

My personal favorites:

"I need a manager who is over the moon happy when I bring in a great order but at the same time is not afraid to kick me in the rear when I need it."

"I don't need a manager, I need a leader."

What comments do you think your AE's would offer?

THERE ARE RICHES IN NICHES

While channel surfing, I stumbled upon a great baseball movie called *Knuckleball!* The movie is set in the 2011 Major League Baseball season and follows the league's only knuckleball pitchers, Tim Wakefield (Boston Red Sox) and R.A. Dickey (New York Mets).

A knuckleball is generally thrown by placing the

tips of the fore and middle fingers along the baseball seams. The pitch, at only about 60 mph, is slow by pro standards when compared to closers who throw over 100 mph. But the ball doesn't spin, creating unpredictable movement, which makes it hard to hit, and often, equally hard to catch.

A quote from the movie describes Wakefield's and Dickey's situations best "… a handful of pitchers in the entire history of baseball (have been) forced to resort to the lowest rung on the credibility ladder in their sport: throwing a ball so slow and unpredictable that no one wants anything to do with it."

This movie was a must-see for my great life-long friend and sports nut, Billy Bruce. After viewing, he responded, "I was thinking while watching that you don't have to be like everyone else to succeed, you just need to find, and never give up on, your niche."

Wakefield and Dickey were able to build strength out of a perceived weakness. They have built careers on a pitch that no sane pitcher in today's game would touch with a *ten*-foot pole. "There are riches in niches," as Jim Doyle would say.

This movie prompted me to reflect on my career in media sales. How many times have I undervalued a sales knuckleballer because he or she was a bit non-traditional when compared to the rest of the team? As a sales manager, do you ever waste time and effort trying to correct a perceived weakness? Would your time be better spent building on strengths?

I can remember struggling with an AE because she consistently fell short on project sales. Her comfort was new business. As a result, she was consistently overachieving her new business budget.

In a desperate move, I dropped her project budget and put in a stretch goal for her new business number. It was such a win-win that we incorporated the strategy with the rest of the sellers: "stretch" budgets for their sales strengths and smaller budgets for their sales weakness categories. There were certainly bumps in the process, and of course, some juggling with the budgets to get in line with corporate expectations, but minimizing sales weaknesses and capitalizing on niche sales strengths paid off.

Take a good look at the sellers on your team. Then, help them determine opportunity and hold them accountable by owning it, and everyone will profit.

In the meantime, make sure to watch the movie *Knuckleball!* I am certain you'll think to yourself, if even for a split second, "60 mph? I could pitch knuckleballs in the majors!"

THE POWER OF TESTIMONIALS

Annually, I sit in on a substantial number of client presentations. Most clients seem to be reasonably engaged while the media AE and sales manager are presenting. However, there's always a new level of focus on each client's face during the video testimonial and success story portion of the presentation.

As I was writing this, an email arrived (I know, turn off the email beep!) from one of our Senior Marketing Consultants. He was sharing news from a television station with an update on a recent presentation. "The client testimonials were the tipping point for this advertiser. He's ready to do business with us!"

From San Diego to Washington, DC, and Lubbock to Sioux Falls, *testimonials close business!* But here's the sad reality. Most sellers in our business don't use testimonials in their presentations!

When I ask, "Why not?" there are a myriad of answers. "We can't get clients to say anything on camera." "We don't want to hurt our relationship by asking." Or, (my personal favorite because all mobile phones now record video), "Our AE's don't want to carry a video camera." Do you know what these answers are called? Excuses.

Do you make excuses for your AE's when it comes to collecting client testimonials?

If I were managing a sales team, I would put in a requirement that all sellers had to turn in at least *one* client video testimonial monthly. By the end of the year, with a staff of *seven* you would have *eighty-four* client video testimonials banked.

Why do I think client testimonials are so important?

1. **They are credible**. The satisfied client is essentially informing a possibly on-the-fence prospect that, "I was once thinking what you might be thinking now. But I took a chance, and as a result my business is better for the decision."

2. **They can say things that a media rep cannot say**. Many times an AE will try to convey to a prospect that their pain is understood. A prospect is suspect of an AE making claims if they haven't walked in the prospect's shoes. In other words, a furniture store owner is more likely to trust comments from a furniture store owner vs. comments from an AE.

3. **They do the heavy lifting**. This is an especially important point for your new AE's. These videos can serve as a valuable presentation filler and can expand on points, making an inexperienced marketing rep look more experienced.

4. **They add color to a presentation**. We're in the entertainment business. Doesn't it make sense to include video in our presentations, especially when they're

informative and entertaining? A half-hour presentation from a monotone rep can seem pretty long. However, a presentation broken up with video testimonials adds variety and interest.

5. **They divert conversation away from ratings and share**. From my experience, any station or cable outlet can talk ratings, share, thousands, etc. The professionals who talk about creative ideas close more business and larger shares of business. Showing video testimonials to clients will naturally move the conversation away from a ratings discussion and into a creative discussion.

The last word on this topic I'll leave to the Executive Vice President of Jim Doyle & Associates, Tom Ray. He addressed the proper time to ask for a video testimonial in one of our *The Money Memo* newsletters: "I absolutely love the off-the-cuff line a Regional VP shared with her sales department while discussing the importance of capturing success videos. She said, 'The curve of gratitude is a nano-second!' In other words, when your client is raving about the success you've delivered, DON'T WAIT! Pull out your smartphone and capture that enthusiasm on video. You never know when one of those random events is going to happen and they change their tune."

CHAPTER 4

SALES PREPARATION AND PLANNING

A goal without a plan is just a wish.
-Antoine de Saint-Exupery

FIVE AREAS WHERE SALESPEOPLE NEED HELP

Before visiting a sales team I make it a habit to contact the sales managers with a few questions to get a feel for the staff. It's a bit of a client diagnosis opportunity to make sure I'll connect with their AEs' needs.

One of the most important questions I'll ask during these conversations is, "Can you tell me where your team needs the most help?" The answers are usually fairly consistent, regardless of market size and location. If your sales stars need improvements in any of these areas, it's up to you, as their leader, to assist with getting them up to speed. If you want to have some fun with this information, assign an AE to each of the following categories and let them direct a sales meeting for the rest of the team on how to improve in each of the shortfalls.

FIVE Areas Where Salespeople Need Help

Poor organizational skills. According to research by office machine company, Brother, an estimated 76 working hours per person each year are lost as a result of disorganization in the workplace. The majority of lost employee time is spent searching for items around desks and offices for misplaced paper files or for documents on computers.

Poor organizational skills can also apply to time management. I was at a station for a week of client calls where an AE gave *two* clients the wrong appointment times. The same AE missed a big client presentation because he couldn't remember the scheduled time. How many chances would a seller of this caliber get on your team?

Time is money and disorganization is *lost* money.

Failure to fill the funnel. This one sometimes isn't spotted until it's too late. You're pleased to see weeks of consistent orders coming from one of your star sellers. Then, for some reason, they hit a slump and new orders are nonexistent. The "slump," more often than not, can be explained in a retrospective review of the last month's call count. Some AE's have a tendency to slow down on call volume when the money is flowing. "Why should I exert myself while

I'm still making budget?" sellers may ask themselves. However, if fresh prospects aren't in line to take the place of converted prospects, billing suffers weeks down the line.

Taking shortcuts. Too many times, sellers skip over critical pieces of diagnosis, which results in money left on the table, or worse yet, money in your competitors' pockets. Sales pro assumptions are the predominant reason that sales shortcuts happen. Sellers "assume" they know the needs or specs on a client and then, without asking, they build a presentation around the wrong assumptions. Teach your team to give the prospect the courtesy of confirming or denying an assumption.

When it comes to presentations, prospects can tell if your AE is prepared. Whether a sure thing or not, clients deserve the whole show. Help your sellers understand that the "whole show" cannot be assembled an hour before the appointment. As college basketball coach Bobby Knight reminds us, *"The will to succeed is important, but what's more important is the will to prepare."*

They lack an understanding of what they're selling. There is no excuse for needing help here. You, as a sales manager, need to train and test every AE until they know your programming and products inside out. To some AE's, selling digital products is intimidating and confusing because it's new to their sales tool box. What these AE's don't understand is that complaining does not help the situation. Digital is not going away. As one VP of Sales said to me, "It's time to get educated or get out."

They don't ask for the order. With the ever increasing demand of cross-platform sales, I see some incredible presentations. Unfortunately, many of these presentations don't end as "sold." Why? Because the AE didn't ask for the order. In some instances, sellers even discourage a prospect's decision with comments like, "You probably need a week or so to think about this..."

The best sales success is always at the table and in the moment. AE's should trained to incorporate closes throughout the presentation, which then lead to a more relaxed "ask" at the conclusion.

Need more to drive the point home to your team? Google clips from the classic sales movie *Glengarry Glen Ross* for your next sales meeting.

Bonus: Wrong attitude. In the spirit of under-promising and over-delivering, here's a 6th bonus to the *5 Areas Where Salespeople Need Help.*

Everyone has a bad day—on occasion. However, when a seller displays a defeatist attitude, they likely lack confidence in the programming or product they're trying to sell. As a result, their attitude has registered virtually a "no sale" before the presentation. They almost want to hear a "no" so that they can come back and spout "I told you so" to the non-believers.

Do you want to know why your dot 2 channel is such a hard sell? It's because your team is accustomed to selling big ratings and they don't believe the dot 2 will deliver results.

Inject end-result benefits and testimonials into your programming and product training. If sales pros have faith in a product, they will passionately and successfully sell it.

AN ANNUAL REMINDER TO FOCUS

At the end of each year, as media sales offices begin conducting their planning and strategy sessions, our organization hears from star sales managers seeking training "juice" to jump-start team performance in the new year.

Generally, before this request, the numbers expectations (budget, local direct, new business, share, etc.) have already been discussed with sellers. The best managers have laid out a vision and steps to ensure new revenue highs.

Certainly, there's renewed excitement in purging the past to make room for new goals. But, at some point, the excitement will level off and some AE's will let off the "sales gas." That's why, when I was in your chair, I liked to host a beginning of the year "FOCUS" themed sales meeting.

What is FOCUS? It's a pinpoint vision of the major priorities that have to be accomplished in order to fulfill the goals at hand. It's a constant awareness of where one is and the definitive next steps one must take in order to achieve what was previously thought to be impossible. Focus is about holding the person in the mirror accountable, *not* getting comfortable, and making a comeback from the inevitable low points that will surface in the upcoming year.

Below are some of the dusted off talking points, in case you'd like to host your own focus-themed sales meeting.

FOCUS

An ability to set goals and to use them every day to guide your actions. Hold yourself accountable!

F

Face calls: Strive for three client face-to-face presentations daily.

Fear of failure: It's okay to fail if we learn from the experience and correct our actions for future improvement. However, failure as a result of lack of preparation is unacceptable. A minimal amount of "fear of failure" will keep you motivated for extra effort and will keep preparation in check.

Fire accounts: Get proactive with your book of business. Who are the prospects burning your daylight and with whom you have a minimal chance, at best, of doing business? Drop them. Consider trading with your sales peers those small billing accounts and clients whose personalities may not sync with your own. Going through this exercise will free your time for bigger money opportunities.

O

Organized: Maximize your selling time by working the money clock. Ask yourself, "Is my effort at this very second making money?"

Optimistic: There is no room for pessimism on this team. If you think you're not getting the sale, guess what, you're not! To quote Thomas Jefferson, "I am a great believer in luck—the harder I work the more I have of it."

Opportunity: Always be on the lookout for opportunity. Instead of pointing fingers, create your own opportunity. Do you monitor the competition? Are you dedicated to self-improvement education? Do you ask for referrals?

C

Competence: Know your programming, specials, ratings, the competition, etc. Business owners want to deal with professionals and winners.

Commitment: You get out what you put in. Blame the person in the mirror for your failure or success. Are you committed to your goals?

Closing: ABC: Always Be Closing. If you don't ask, you don't get.

U

Unforgettable: Customers appreciate premium treatment and tell their business associates, who then become referrals! Build a reputation as the best media sales professional in the city.

Unrelenting: Do not diminish in intensity, speed or effort. Do you have what it takes to be number one?

Upset: Get mad when another station, outlet or media takes *your* money. Beat them to the next client. What's on your competitor's list that you will soon control?

S

Service: Building customers for long-term relationships is the only way to achieve your financial goals.

System: Not everyone is alike. Utilize available tools and experiences to create your own. Your system builds the framework for maximizing goal achievement.

Success: Always maintain hard work and an eye on the goal. This is not easily achieved. If it were painless, everyone could do it!

A SOMETIMES OVERLOOKED REVENUE CATEGORY

While waiting in line with a hungry brunch crowd, I met a local church treasurer. He noticed my local television station golf shirt and began to excitedly explain his recent positive experience with television advertising.

Apparently, one of the parishioners had a connection to the lowest rated television station in the market. This member "aggravated" the church board to meet with the station TV rep to discuss television advertising. After the meeting, the board was surprisingly in full support of moving forward with a three-month marketing plan. It should be noted that the plan consisted of thirty-second commercials to be aired during inexpensive weekday/daytime programming. The church had just over 170 members.

The treasurer fully anticipated the marketing experiment would prove to be a waste of money. His expectation was correct, at least until the third week of the commercial flight. That was the week the assembly welcomed the first guests, who were moved to visit the church by the pastor's television invitation. In the following weeks, the number of visitors continued to increase. At the end of the three-month contract, the congregation had grown just over 20%. As a result, the church board happily rewarded the TV station with a contract renewal.

It's a pretty good bet your team of sales pros could improve your revenue line by helping a few churches take advantage of the power of your airwaves. Below are a few tips to maximize this sometimes overlooked revenue category:

- TV and radio stations might title your block of Sunday morning religious half-hours and sell sponsorships with ten-second open and close billboards, i.e., "First Methodist Church proudly supports WEGD's Sunday Morning Devotions." Instead of an announcer, feature the sponsor pastor reading the open and close. On TV, utilize the bottom third of the screen for key service times and contact information.
- Half-hour paid programming slots have a minute-and-a-half end break. Assuming you reserve thirty seconds of each end break for promotions, that leaves two minutes of inventory for each hour. A three-hour paid religious block provides six minutes of commercial inventory or twelve thirty-second avails. Create long-term packages of four commercials to sell to three churches.
- Have news? Produce a once-a-week sponsored segment that airs (the same time in every Saturday night news) and features the sponsored church's "parishioner of the week."
- For cable outlets that don't have news? Create a similar parishioner-of-the-week sponsored segment and air it in the same slot every week. Promote it to make it an event, "Tune-in every Saturday at 7:58pm as Second Baptist Church spotlights its parishioner of the week."
- Help churches capitalize on peak attendance

times of the year—Easter and Christmas. Create a twenty-second open/close donut. Call it "Jesus Is The Reason For The Season." The creative should feature the pastor of each sponsor church inviting viewers to attend the numerous planned holiday services.

- Get creative with testimonials from church members. Doing so will develop cheerleaders and a positive buzz among the flock.
- Lastly, don't overlook the generosity of well-heeled members of the congregation. These individuals may be more than happy to contribute extra dollars to assist the church with its marketing goals.

CLOSE MORE BUSINESS WITH THE RIGHT SUIT COLOR

Have you ever received professional dress questions from your sales team? The industry standard advises our appearance should be one notch above the client. Why? Your sales star may have difficulty establishing quick rapport sporting their most expensive suit-and-tie combo when meeting with the local HVAC owner/operator dressed in his work-worn uniform.

That very situation is not uncommon. When a blue collar client takes a break from the dirty jobsite to talk business, smart sellers will take off jackets and loosen ties to lessen the impact of clothing differences.

Dressing for the occasion is pretty much common sense, but have you ever given thought to the impact that color may have on your team's sales success? Research of the all-important "first impression" indicates that color trumps shape and texture for creating emotional impact. Many sales are lost because the business owner feels the presenter doesn't "look the part."

According to professional clothier Gregg Shawen, of the Tom James Company, there are five recognized suit-color categories. As a general rule, the darker the color the higher the perception of authority. The color black epitomizes authority. Stripes add power to any color and plaids convey a casual feel.

Below is a brief overview of the five suit categories:

NAVY: Conveys confidence. The wearer is perceived as trustworthy, intelligent, and stable. Wear navy for presentations and when meeting with a first-time client. This is the best color for negotiating.

CHARCOAL GRAY: Wearers of this color are viewed as mature, practical, and sophisticated. AE's concerned about the perception of being "too young" should wear this shade. Charcoal is a good suit choice when picking up client checks. It's also a good color for contract renewal appointments and for meetings with your boss.

BLUE-GRAY: This color projects a firm but fair image. Managers should wear this shade for recruiting, interviewing, and hiring. Account executives should consider blue-gray suits when trying to earn a client's trust and respect.

LIGHT GRAY: Wearers are perceived as confident and charismatic. This shade is good for all-day client appointments and for staff meetings. The color is the most casual of the five categories.

EARTH TONES: This category includes most browns, tans, and olives. It's great for building rapport as the wearer is perceived as sympathetic and down-to-earth. Earth tones are a great pick for meeting with an unhappy client, seeing a small business owner or for conducting employee reviews. (www.tomjames.com)

IS YOUR TEAM SELLING THE DRILL BIT OR THE HOLE?

If you're a television viewer (and you should be because after all you're in the business) you have no doubt seen the increase in commercials touting supplementation for men with low testosterone. This once taboo subject is going mainstream, thanks to drug companies utilizing the power of your airwaves and cable feeds to educate consumers.

My eleven-year-old son, Evan, and I were watching television when one of the latest low-T commercials interrupted our college football game. The product was Axiron (here's a lead for your sales team to give a local doctor a competitive advantage.) It was the first roll-on testosterone cream. One applies it daily, just like deodorant. "Wow," I thought to myself, "What a great product for those afraid of needles."

Evan, on the other hand, was thinking something entirely different. He asked, "Why in that commercial do they show everyone smiling and having fun?" Evan had observed something that Axiron's marketing is doing right. They're selling the hole, not the drill bit.

You may have heard Jim Doyle explaining this concept. Let's assume you have a need for a 2-inch hole in a wall in your house. The reason is unimportant, but for the sake of argument, you need the hole to run some plumbing. Upon going to the toolbox, you discover that you don't have the right bit to drill the hole. As a result, you now make a trip to the hardware store to purchase a 2-inch drill bit. But aren't you really buying a 2-inch hole? The drill bit is simply a tool to get the hole—a means to an end.

In Axiron's commercial, they weren't advertising just testosterone. They were playing to the consumer's "want," by advertising a chance for men with low testosterone to get their lives back. The smiles are a direct reflection of how supplementing with testosterone (drill bit) can return one's life back to a fulfilled life of enjoyment (the hole).

Many times, we see creative commercials that look great and might even win production awards, but they're not effective in moving product. These commercials often don't address a client's Unique Selling Proposition (USP), and worse yet, they don't contain a call to action. These types of messages merely address the drill bit.

Think of your sales team for a moment. Are they selling the drill bit or the hole? AE's who understand this results-oriented concept write more business, renew more contracts, and in general, are more successful.

Did Evan understand the drill bit and hole analogy? Maybe. I took his response of, "I got it Dad," while his eyes never left the TV, as positive affirmation; moving him one step closer to a career in marketing.

LOOK PAST THE "I" IN YOUR THANK YOU

A thank you letter from someone who worked on our house arrived via snail mail. *Impressive,* I thought, since many don't utilize the power of a thank you any longer, let alone a thank you via regular mail. After reading the letter I was a bit turned off and the "happy feeling" window of intent was totally lost on me. Why? In three paragraphs of writing, "I" was used thirteen times. In fact, each of the three paragraphs started with "I." It was apparent to me that the thank you was not sincere and was less about being thankful and more about the owner and securing future business.

When was the last time you reviewed your sales team's client correspondence? Or maybe the bigger question is, "Do you expect your account executives to thank clients in writing?" If not, maybe you should reconsider.

As a manager, you no doubt understand the importance of positive differentiation from the competition. The easiest way for your stars to get noticed, to build rapport, and to get a jump-start on building long-term relationships is through a *hand written* thank you. Conversely, emailing your appreciation shows a lack of initiative and classifies you as average.

When writing a client thank you, consider using "I" only when absolutely necessary. This will help direct the tone of your thoughts to customer-centered—not self-centered. Look for opportunities to substitute "we" or "us" in place of "I" to extend the feeling of team.

In general, your correspondence should have *three* components:

1. **An open "opportunity" thanks**

2. **Appreciation for the business and a "help" offer**

3. A positive wish or close

What follows is a "short and sweet" thank you that can be customized per your relationship with your client.

Dear Dave,

Thank you for allowing CBS 14 the opportunity to contribute to your marketing strategy.

We appreciate your investment, confidence and partnership in our station, and encourage you to rely upon us for any assistance that may aid you in exceeding your advertising goals.

Best to you and your staff for a record (current or future year)!

Sincerely,
John

For added impact, write the letter on your company's branded notecards and always include *your* business card, even if the client already has your card. This will make it easy for the client to pass your contact information on to an associate who may need your marketing expertise.

SELLING TO BIRTH ORDER

Many years ago, I was intrigued by a book from Dr. Kevin Leman (www.drleman.com) titled, *The Birth Order Book: Why You Are the Way You Are.* In it,

Leman reveals four personality types resulting from one's birth order: first born, only child, middle child, and last born. The book was a real eye-opener in explaining family dynamics and interaction with others. Quickly, I realized how the study of birth order could be a valuable tool for sellers in establishing rapport and positioning for positive presentation feedback, in turn, increasing sales.

This topic is a lot of fun in sales meetings as individual's claim, "That's not me!" while the rest of the room laughs, "Yes it is!" You'll hear a lot of out loud thinking and see brain light bulbs going off as members of your team begin to connect dots and gain clarity on their client relationships.

Utilizing Dr. Leman's four personality types, here are my suggestions on how to best approach each in a sales environment. Feel free to use the following as a conversation starter in your sales meeting.

Selling To Only Children & First Born

Keep in mind when speaking with a first born, you're talking to Mr. or Ms. "No Nonsense." Proceed with caution. He/she is not likely to be impressed with flashy six-color brochures and grand claims. The first born wants to know:

- What is your product or service going to do for me?

- How much does it cost me?

They likely will ask many "Why? What? When? Where?" and "How much?" questions.

Presenting:

Arrive a few minutes early. Get to the point. Follow a plan. Don't ramble or try to fake it. Say your piece—preferably in *five* minutes, *three* would be better. First borns are impressed by efficiency and concern for their time and busy schedule. Don't try to get chummy, just get it done and get out.

Try not to ask the first born any *why* questions. "Why?" is confrontational and puts the other person on the defensive. A question beginning with *why* is a threat to his/her control. First borns like to be in control and they're not pleased by surprises or questions that may put them on the defensive.

Appeal to the ego, avoid insincere flattery, offer plenty of detail, and impress with in-depth research about his/her company. This proves you did your homework before the appointment.

Closing:

Use the psychological principle of "oppositional attraction." (The basis is interaction with a toddler. If you move *toward* the average *two*-year-old, saying, "Come here. Come to me," he/she will run in the opposite direction. But if you want the average *two*-year-old to come to you, you *back up* and say, "Come here." There's something about backing up that gives the child a feeling of control and they're not as fearful.)

Oppositional attraction, as applied to client decision makers in a sales environment, allows you to move toward the close while reminding the first born client that he/she is in control and is the one making the decision. This is done by stating the obvious pluses and minuses. For example, "You have been using WXYZ for eight years and they've provided you with good service. I'd be lying if I said only our station provides better service; lots of companies do. What I'm excited about is the match of our viewers to your target. The Sun Coast residents have been very generous in their viewing support of our channels. As a result, we've established ourselves with your competitors as a valuable partner in their marketing plans."

Selling To Middle Born

Sales are relational to the middle born, as they typically go outside the family first to find friends and groups where they feel somewhat in control and not squeezed, as they do at home. They are good team players—reliable, steady, and loyal. They may take longer to sell, thanks to extended periods of relationship building. However, with fair treatment and service, middle borns tend to be more loyal customers.

Presenting:

Middle borns enjoy being asked many questions.

In fact, the more the better, as they were never asked many questions growing up at home. He/she was simply ignored.

Most middle born clients tend to be laid-back. In rare instances, you can run into a middle born buzz saw. This customer is competitive, aggressive, shy, quiet, and a loner who avoids relationships.

When arranging appointments with the relationship-hungry middle born, ask them if there's anybody else they would like to bring to the meeting, conversation or lunch. A third party sometimes puts the middle born at ease, as the conversation flows easier. Allow the middle born to make this decision, because although they like relationships, it has to be on their terms.

Do everything you can to make your call less a sales call and more a social contact. The middle born often responds to a presentation slower and more sensitively than a first born would. Leave the impression that you're not selling on the first call as much as you're just trying to make a contact and get to know each other.

An effective approach to middle borns is to ask them to describe their biggest business problem or hurdle, i.e., "What's the greatest difficulty you face in business today?" Make sure the solution to solve this problem is central in your follow-up presentation.

Middle borns are not as afraid of change as first

borns may be. They want to be serviced, like in relationship building, and are seeking the warm and fuzzy that helps them feel more secure and at ease with you as their business partner.

Closing:

Establishing and maintaining a relationship are key. If you don't have a relationship, your chances for a "yes" are minimal.

An offer of a money-back guarantee or no-obligation promise is particularly attractive to the middle born. Emphasize how they can check with others about your claims and tell them how you will specifically service them. Testimonials add credibility and provide the middle born the comfort to give you a "yes."

Congratulate and reinforce their decision to invest in your products. *Always* let them know their business is appreciated.

Selling To Last Born

Be as fun and charming as you can and be aware that as the winds change, the last born can change as well. They fly by the seat of their pants and they never stay put for very long.

Often, last borns are more relational than middle borns. They flock to social settings and like to work hard and play hard. Sometimes they like to do both at the same time.

Presenting:

Last born customers love to hear or tell a good story or joke. Ask, "Would you tell me some of your favorite stories—things that have happened in your business? I'd love to hear them."

Be aware of time as stories are shared. Last borns may occupy your sales time with stories, thus prohibiting you from getting to the presentation before they move on to another appointment.

Mention highly visible people or businesses that are advertising with your company, as last borns are very susceptible to being impressed by name-dropping.

Closing:

A typical last born is 180 degrees from the typical first born. Last borns could care less about numbers and graphs. Provide them with flash and glitter in the form of full-color visuals and brochures, as this is how they arrive at the bottom line.

When it comes to weighing the business side against the personal pluses and minuses of a sale, the last born will give the personal side significant weight. The last born tends to ask him/herself, "What does this thing really do for *me*? Does it make *me* feel good?"

Last borns tend to be risk-takers, which is an advantage to the seller during the close. Last borns are spontaneous and tend to want to act now, not later. Do not hesitate to ask for a commitment or a signature. A last born's inclination to risk invites a seller to be more confrontational and a little harder pressing for a decision.

212 DEGREES

My daughter, Madison, and I were attending her freshman orientation at the Pine View School, (www.sarasotacountyschools.net/schools/pineview) which was, at the time, ranked 6th in the nation by *U.S. News*. Would you believe this is a public school?!

I don't know about you, but looking back on my high school experience, I'm guessing my school didn't break the top few thousand in national ranking. As a result, I walked around the Pine View campus in jaw dropping, absolute amazement. The environment was ripe with motivation, achievement, success, etc.,—all the adjectives that you would love to use to describe your sales team environment.

But here's the kicker. Everything displayed or discussed at Pine View was woven with personal accountability. As in, "We're here to give you the tools, but if you fall short because you didn't commit all of your effort, there is only one person to blame." Wow. That's a message that sometimes seems the minority in today's society.

In the television sales business, getting a team

to achieve sales success is not rocket science. A team is motivated by encouragement and training and tools that enable consistent performance excellence. Ultimately, the best performers on the team are harder on themselves than any outside influence could ever be. They compete against themselves for higher and higher achievement.

This thought is driven home with Pine View's philosophy statement:

At 211 degrees, water is hot.

At 212 degrees, it boils.

And with boiling water, comes steam.

And with steam, you can power a train.

One degree more = Exponential Results

Here's a video link explaining 212 Degrees for your sales meeting: (http://play.simpletruths.com/movie/212-the-extra-degree)

THE BEST TIME TO MAKE COLD CALLS

When it comes to cold calling prospects, I've lost count of the number of excuses heard on why "x" day or "y" time is *not* good to reach out to a potential client. In my early sales days, I wasn't immune to delivering a few of these whoppers to a manager. Things like, "They surely won't take a call Monday morning while they're getting ready for the week," or "I can't call Friday because it might interrupt their weekend preparation," or how about, "Calling between 11:30am and 2pm is not effective because the business owner takes lunch around that time."

Over the years, I've developed an attitude that any time a client picks up the phone and engages is a good time to prospect. In other words, there is no better or worse day or time to make cold calls.

That thought process was proven wrong upon discovering recent research. According to a study from www.insightsquared.com there is indeed a best time of day and best time of the week to make cold calls. They arrived at this conclusion after analyzing over 10,000 sales calls and determining the highest prospect connect rate.

The best time of day to cold call is between 10am and 4pm. This is counter to conventional thinking that calling early in the morning and at the end of the work day yields the greatest results. In fact, the start of the work day delivers a 5% connection rate, while the 10a-4p connection rate hovers just above 8%. There's a sharp decline in connection rate after 4pm.

The best day of the week to cold call is Tuesday. The connection rate with prospects on this day achieves 10%. All subsequent days decline from Tuesday's high, with the lowest connect rate, 8.7%, being Friday. So, Tuesday between 10a and 4p is the best time for cold calling.

The small percentage difference may not seem like a lot until one considers the net effect of connection rate improvements spread across multiple calls throughout the week. Quite simply, even a slight improvement will result in multiple, additional selling opportunities.

Still skeptical? Why not test the study by asking your AE's to reach out to prospects mid-morning and to use the late afternoon for research and sales meetings. Then, compare the results to your current prospect conversion ratios. According to the study, you might be surprised.

A COUNTER VIEW TO SILENCE AS A SALES TOOL

In your next sales meeting, quiz your team on what they should do the second after they ask a prospect to make a purchase decision. If your sellers have been trained properly, they'll know that the response is some form of "shut up" or "go silent." Inevitably, as that answer is bantered about, someone in the room will add a post script from years ago training, "Yeah, because the first one to speak loses."

I disagree.

In the not-so-distant past, many sales trainers suggested that silence should be used as a pressure tool. They promoted fast-talking presentations accompanied by tie-down statements designed to corner a customer so that they have no out and feel pressured into a "yes," which was the only foreseeable way to escape the uncomfortable situation. From this grew the thought process that the first one to speak loses. The non-verbals conveyed with this promotion of silent pressure— leaning forward in the chair and staring at the client, almost willing them to hurry up with their "yes"— can result in a negative air in the room.

A couple of by-products from this style of training are buyer's remorse, which results in cancellations, and in general, a poor public stigma associated with the word *sales.*

Please do not misunderstand. I am *not* saying silence has no role in the sales process. However, my belief is counter to the use of silence as a pressure tool. Silence should be offered out of respect for the customer.

You see, the customer has given their time to listen and participate in a presentation that is likely filled with concepts, strategies and marketing tools, many of which the potential client is seeing for the first time. If your sellers are seasoned, they will ask for a large stretch investment backed up with a solid return on investment explanation. The presentation could be lengthy, maybe as long as an hour. To put it another way, your AE is giving a ton of info to the client in a very short window. The decision on whether or not to move forward could have substantial repercussions on the future of the client's business. As a result, the business owner may need to marinate for a few minutes to get their head wrapped around everything that was just put before them.

After the "ask" for the business, encourage your AE's to smile, lean back in their chair, and sit quietly and patiently while the potential client considers the options. These non-verbals promote an air of comfort, almost as if to say, "Take your time. I know that's a lot to consider."

For your AE's who you suspect may be uncomfortable with silence, I have a suggestion. In a sales meeting, tell everyone that for the length of the meeting, any time a question is asked, the respondent has to wait 10 seconds before providing an answer. At first, 10 seconds will seem, for some, like an eternity. However, the wait will seem shorter and less intimidating the longer and more times the game is played.

An All-In Sales System

Elise Kephart is the Vice President of Training for Phone Ninjas (www.phoneninjas.com), a phone sales training company that specializes in training automotive sellers. She is nationally recognized as the "The YouTube Diva" who has sold thousands of cars through her individually customized, unique, persuasive and marketing videos.

Elise was interviewed in one of our *The Leaders Edge* management coaching tele-seminars, in which she shared in detail her successful method of getting to decision makers. Her process is deliberate and methodical, and it creates results. A review of her system would be a great topic for discussion at your next sales meeting.

As a young auto sales professional, she realized that in order to be successful she had to be "different" from the other salespeople. Her desire to be different spawned a successful system of prospecting that combines multi-touch points to break through and get noticed among all the other vendors vying for a prospect's attention. She has refined the approach over the years and today employs the same system while reaching out to auto dealer decision makers to discuss Phone Ninja services. Here's her system:

Step 1. First thing in the morning, place a phone call. Leave a voicemail if they don't pick up. In the VM, introduce yourself and give them a reason to call you back. For example, "I have an idea that I saw at our sister station that will dramatically increase your business," and then set the stage that you will be following up throughout the course of the day if you don't hear back from them.

Step 2. Send a video email; this differentiates you from others calling and provides the emotion that letters on a screen fail to convey. It's easy to do with a smartphone. The video can be a message as simple as, "Hey Jim, my name is John at KRMV. I just left a voicemail for you and wanted to share this video so that you know who's on the other end of the computer. I'm in a position to help you and I have a few quick questions and some information that has the ability to increase your business. My number is 941-926-7355. It's close to 10am on Thursday. I'll be available for your call until 5pm today. If I don't hear from you in the next few hours, I'll follow up with you later today. Before you go, I've added a few video testimonials from satisfied customers for you to enjoy." You can use YouTube to post this as private video and supply a link to the video in your email. Additionally, you can use a YouTube tool to watermark your phone number over the video.

Step 3. Send a text or email with something like, "Hey Jim, I just sent you a video email and left a voicemail earlier. I realize that sometimes video emails get sent to spam and wanted you to have access to the message that was specially created for you. I'll check in later if I don't hear from you. Again, it's John at 941-926-7355." If you like, you can also add your video link to the text.

Step 4. Send a VIP packet via US Postal Mail. This includes a cover letter, your bio showing some kind of service or passion for what you do, client testimonials, and any awards for which you, and/or your media outlet, may be known.

To this point, the above four steps should be completed in about two hours. It's in these two hours that the foundation of communication and intent is built with your prospect.

Step 5. About 11am, place another phone call to the prospect. However, on this call, do not leave a voicemail. Elise stated that, unless the prospect picks up, she is simply trying to get the decision maker to make note of an unrecognized number when they check their mobile or office "missed call" list. Clients have returned her call just out of curiosity because they didn't recognize the number.

Step 6. Send another email follow-up after the phone call. Something like, "Hey Jim, I just tried to reach you again. Please call me at 941-926-7355 when you have a quick moment today. I'll check in again if I haven't heard from you in a few hours."

Steps 7 and 8. Two hours after the last email, repeat steps 5 and 6.

Step 9. Fourth and final phone call for the day. If you still get voicemail, leave a message similar to, "Hey Jim, it's John at KRMV 941-926-7355. I've been trying to reach you today and have some great news on what we can accomplish for you. Again, please call me when you have a moment, 941-926-7355. I'll be here until 5pm today."

The next day the whole process gets repeated (except for the VIP mailing.) Always follow up each phone call attempt with an email.

Elise states that in virtually every case, she gets a return call from a prospect no later than the *third* day. The clients now have evidence that you follow up as you say you will and they have, by the third day, received the VIP packet. They now understand that they're not dealing with the average sales rep.

Does Elise's "all-in" sales system seem like a lot of work? Absolutely. But then again, the most successful sellers put in the effort to do the work that others will not do or are not capable of doing.

It's Time for a Presentation Review

No matter which airline you fly, each is mandated to conduct a pre-flight safety briefing. If you're like me, the safety briefing is an opportunity to finish up a last-second phone call, arrange under-the-seat baggage or read the paper. Regardless of the airline, it seems that this is the attitude of 80% or more of travelers. Why? Maybe we've heard it too many times before, or maybe it's because the delivery, in general, is a pretty standard monotone script of "grasp the buckle, pull tight on the belt, etc." It's just not compelling enough to hold our attention.

A couple of years ago, I recall hearing about a Southwest Airlines flight attendant who "rapped" the pre-flight safety briefing. There was even one who sang the briefing. In my travels, I haven't run into either of those creative deliveries, but as of late, Delta has been impressive with their video efforts. In fact, Delta's briefing videos are so good that I often put down the paper to view the briefing, laughing along with fellow passengers. You can find Delta's safety video collection via a Google search.

So what does Delta do right in their videos? The first thing is that they realized they needed to differentiate from the norm to get noticed. Secondly, they used humor throughout the presentation. Lastly, their creative is memorable.

As a sales manager, do you take the time to periodically review your team's presentations? I see too many presentations that look alike. Many are one-sided—too much about the station or cable outlet and not enough about the client. Unfortunately, the majority of these presentations lack creativity and client customization. A healthy percentage of these presentations don't even contain an "ask" for the order!

Here's a sales meeting idea to make your team the Delta of the market. Have each AE bring in their best client presentation. Without the AE pitching, have the group grade the presentations on content and look. Ask, "Do our presentations look like the same old 'dog and pony' show?" The results will provide an opportunity to discuss improvements. Before the meeting ends, don't forget to deep-seed your minimum expectations like customer-centric points, station branding, video testimonials, and an annual "ask" for the business.

CHAPTER 5

WITHOUT CUSTOMERS YOU HAVE NO BUSINESS

You're not listening. I'm telling you what I need to give you money and you are not listening. -David Newman

IGNORING A CUSTOMER'S COMPLAINT IS A HUGE MISTAKE

While standing in the National car rental line, I could not believe my ears. A competing rental car company, Alamo, was within earshot of National's counter. The conversation between the Alamo rep and a customer was as follows:

Customer: *I rented a car from you 2 days ago. A couple of hours ago, I noticed the car was leaking a lot of oil and making a funny noise. I left my family at the beach and immediately drove the car back here to exchange it. One of your lot guys is looking at the car now.*

Alamo rep: *How many miles did you drive the*

car?

Customer: *I'm not sure. We've been taking in the local sights and going from the condo to the beach. It has been in-town driving.*

Alamo rep: *Did you return the car with a full tank of gas?*

Customer (now getting a little heated): *The car sounds like it's a block from breaking down and you want me to stop for gas?!*

Alamo rep: *You signed a contract stating that when you returned the car it would have a full tank of gas. There will be a charge to you for the cost of filling up the vehicle...*

At this point, the customer turns three shades of red and unloads on the rental car rep with words that are not fit for this writing.

What just happened here? I'm guessing Alamo just lost a customer for life.

The rental company's car was faulty. There are so many things the rep could have done to massage the inconvenience the customer was experiencing. The first step should have been a sincere apology and a reassurance that the problem will quickly get fixed. Maybe an upgrade car could have been offered. Unfortunately, the rep did neither and instead chose to focus on collecting gas money.

When one of your clients is upset over a legitimate AE mistake, how do your sellers handle the situation? My hope is that they first apologize and take the complaint seriously, and then immediately go about fixing the wrong and trying to win back the client's trust.

If the situation is something the AE cannot handle, they will likely come to you for help. Your role is to set the example for your sales pro by immediately calling the client to smooth over the situation. Clients will appreciate contact from a manager who's taking responsibility and is re-confirming the importance of the relationship. Many times, if handled correctly, this call can turn a mistake into a giant win for the company.

My second year as an account executive, our traffic department scheduled Memorial Day copy for a furniture store's July 4th weekend sale. The first thing Monday morning, the furniture store owner called to unload her disappointment on me.

I immediately got the LSM involved, who called the owner to apologize. As soon as the LSM finished the call, we hopped into his car, picked up two dozen doughnuts, and drove to the furniture store. We walked straight to the owner's office and delivered the doughnuts and a card with this written message: *Mistakes happen, but that's no excuse for running the wrong copy for your weekend sale. There will be no charge for the "wrong copy" commercials. In addition, we will add a bonus, matching schedule to your next weekend sale. We absolutely appreciate and value your business and we apologize for the inconvenience to you and your staff.*

At the end of the week, the client added money to her commercial schedule—proof that our sincere apology worked and that she was able to move forward with our relationship as though the mistake had never happened.

A SALES MAINTENANCE REMINDER

Recently, I took my car in for maintenance. How did I know it was time for maintenance? The car dealer sent me a postcard reminder. Wouldn't it be great if someone sent media professionals a sales maintenance reminder? Today, I'm skipping the reminder and delivering to you *seven* sales maintenance tips that are sure to tune up your interactions with clients.

- **Be Yourself.** This makes you appear more trustworthy and natural in your presentation. Clients can spot "fake" a mile away.
- **Play to Your Personality Strengths and Weaknesses.** Understand how to capitalize and benefit from your personality type. For example, are you shy? If so, you're going to have to push yourself to make client deposits to get the appointment. If you're outgoing, you may need to dial back on the personality if you're dealing with a timid buyer.

- **Be Prepared.** Do not waste a client's time by making up the presentation on the spot. This is your chance to make the intangible come to life. Make the process fun for both the client and you.
- **Don't Present Like A Robot.** It's great that you know your PowerPoint like the back of your hand. However, leave a little brain room to convey your enthusiasm, passion, and entertainment skills during the presentation. Clients want to deal with people, not robots!
- **Listen With Your Eyes.** Observe the feedback signals your client sends during your presentation, and adjust accordingly. Be aware that at the same time they're gauging your responses.
- **Combine Knowledge with Friendliness.** Most clients like to buy from media stars who are knowledgeable and friendly. Note that "friendly" is second. That's because friendly may get you in the door, but your problem-solving knowledge for the client is what will earn you an invitation to stay. Empty presentations that are heavy on friendly and short on knowledge will earn you a friendly "no."
- **Love What You Do.** You're in the right career if you can cross off more good than bad days. When you're having fun it creates an

energy that feeds others. Ideas come to you faster and are more plentiful when you're happy and loving what you do.

SIGNS AND THE MESSAGES THEY CONVEY TO CUSTOMERS

At the risk of showing your age, raise your hand if you remember the 1970's hit song "Signs." The Five Man Electric Band, a Canadian rock group, recorded the song that featured lyrics with themes of exclusion.

During a visit to a local restaurant, it occurred to me that there are clients, some of them probably doing business with your outlet, who unknowingly build walls of unfriendly customer service simply by posting signs. The messages tend to add convenience for the business operator and *not* the customer.

Here are a few signs that greeted me at the pizzeria counter when I went to place my order:
- Restrooms are for customers only
- No bills larger than a twenty
- Absolutely no cell phone usage at counter
- Refills are twenty-five cents
- Outdoor seating for pizzeria diners only

Ironically, every one of the signs was within three feet of the countertop tip jar!

It is vitally important to win trust if someone wants to be seen by clients as customer-focused.

Encountering a wall of hand-written, typed, colored, and black and white messages of what one cannot do, before even having a chance to place an order, does not come off as very customer-focused.

The Five Man Electric Band taught us to sing, "Sign, sign, everywhere a sign. Blockin' out the scenery, breakin' my mind. Do this, don't do that, can't you read the sign?" Remind your clients that putting up a fence of unfriendly signs at their business alienates customers and ultimately results in lost revenue.

THE TRUMP CARD IN ALL SALES SCENARIOS

"We used to do business with a handshake, face-to-face. Now it's a phone call and a fax, we'll get back to you later, with another fax probably… Well folks, something's got to change. We're going to set out for a little face-to-face chat with every customer we have."

These lines are excerpts from an award-winning 1990 United Airlines commercial. Unfortunately, if you substitute email and text for the word fax, these sentences and their application in the TV ad sales world resonate even louder some 24 years later. But why?

In an effort to make us more productive and efficient, technology improvements have taken away or minimized the "social" interaction in relationships. It's ironic, actually, that we would choose machines over social interaction because the root of all selling—the foundation to sales success—starts with a relationship with the economic decision maker.

Too often, sellers utilize email, texts, phone messages, etc.—anything but an in-person meeting—to shield themselves from rejection and ultimately a lost sale. These AE's never develop a buyer/seller relationship. As a result, they never realize their full sales potential. They are the first to get cancelled or shorted during budget cuts. Why would a salesperson expect anything else when the individual controlling the checkbook can't even name their rep?

Over 90% of communication is nonverbal. One can't read nonverbal communication in an email. People like to buy from those who share common interests. Some of that will come through via phone conversations. But phone pitches are a long-shot, second to digesting affirmations in person while scanning the office to connect common interest dots.

By the way, there is no better time than now if it's been a while since you've made an in-person management deposit with a loyal client. Don't give them a chance to feel their business is being taken for granted. Good luck trying to get a meeting after the client cancels an agreement.

Technology affords us access to background on

individuals like never before. But this information should be an aid to the sales process, not a replacement, because the trump card in all sales scenarios is still, when possible, an eyeball-to-eyeball presentation. As a television sales manager, it's important to reinforce this concept with your team and equally important for you to be a friendly, recognized face among your sellers' key clients.

ENCOURAGE YOUR SELLERS TO BE CLIENT CUPIDS

On Valentine's Day, besides picking out the right card or gift for your partner, family or significant other, did you do anything special for the folks in your office?

Valentine's Day is a great day to extend a bit of love to your sales team with a small token of appreciation. As a General Sales Manager, I used to pass out individual roses (the color yellow for friendship) and chocolates to the sales staff. Later, as General Manager, I extended the giving to the entire station. (Admittedly, there was a bit of double-dipping as the roses were purchased from an AE selling flowers in support of his Lions Club charity.) Regardless, the practice resulted in lots of smiles and feel good moments and is something I still enjoy doing at our office headquarters in Sarasota.

No doubt, a few of your star AE's take advantage of the Valentine's Day holiday by designating themselves a sort of "Client Cupid," delivering candies to clients. While this can be fun for both the advertiser and AE, there are other ways for your sellers to achieve Client Cupid status beyond February 14th:

Client Deposits. You've likely heard me say, "AE's have to make a deposit before making a withdrawal." Deposits are not as easy as concert ticket drop-ins. The client has to feel as though each sales star has taken a more than casual interest in the success of their business. How do members of your team accomplish this? The first step is to acquire a unique understanding of the advertiser's business. This is achieved through diagnosis. In the follow-up presentation, your AE should address how to satisfy the specific challenges, needs, and goals.

Whether doing business with a client or not, your AE's should regularly extend sincere offers of assistance or information. Teach them to *share the love* with clients and prospects through industry articles, videos, testimonials, research, case studies or anything that helps create or continue a business owner's positive momentum.

A Written Thank You. This is a no-brainer, and writing them should be required of all sales team members. Many sales managers across the country realize the value of sending "thank you's" and will reward contest points or tie top seller performance contests or bonus plans to proof of a minimum number of "thank you's" sent.

There are multiple levels or opportunities to express <u>written</u> appreciation. Notice I said *written.* An emailed message lacks creativity, doesn't stand out, and falls short when trying to establish a professional impression.

Over the course of growing a business from a prospect to a client, they could receive a written thanks as many as a half dozen or more times in the first year:

1. **After the diagnosis meeting**
2. **After the presentation**
3. **From the AE after the close**
4. **From a manager after the close**
5. **After a significant AE or company award or ratings victory, e.g., "Our success is only possible because of your support..."**
6. **At the end of the year in a letter from the GM**

Nothing shows love like a sincere thank you for a business partnership.

Beneficial Introductions. To build a strong local direct foundation, your sellers need to be on the lookout for business owners who could benefit simply by knowing each other. For example, common sense would dictate that personal injury attorneys and chiropractors could help one another. Many lawsuits result from car wrecks and many car wrecks cause back injuries.

Average-to-good account executives recognize this connection and may offer a contact phone number to one or the other. However, elite sellers will schedule a business lunch for the threesome to personally introduce the attorney and chiropractor. Many years later, as the attorney and chiropractor reflect upon the origin of their relationship, which Client Cupid will they remember as being in the middle and bringing them together? Your AE!

ASSUMPTIONS AND CUSTOMER SERVICE SURVEYS DO NOT MIX

During a mad dash to the airport, I made a quick Taco Bell detour. Fast food is not typically high on my preference list, but I was in a rush, the drive-thru was open, and there was no waiting.

After spewing "Hello?" three times into the drive-up speaker, someone, who had obviously been inconvenienced, answered with, "Yes?" Not a, "Can I help you?" or, "Would you like to try...?" but a stern, "Yes?"

I placed my order, which ended *without* a total, further instructions or even a thank you from the other side. I decided to roll the dice and pull up to the second window. Surprisingly, the order was packaged and quickly passed through my car window. After collecting the change, I again noted the absence of a thank you and started to pull away. About 10 yards past the drive-thru window I was startled by a Taco Bell employee hanging out the window, waving her arms and yelling, "You forgot this!"

A copy of "this" is below, exactly as it was handed to me, complete with yellow hi-lites, "Dorito" misspelling, and ripped edges. It serves as an example of how a company tries to improve the customer experience through customer feedback. However, in this example, there's a disconnect between intent and the way the request for feedback is executed.

> **Tell The Bell**   #024556
> *We love our customers, let us know how much you love us!*
> *We value your opinion. Let us know how amazing your cashier*
> *Briton was and how delicious your food was. You can call/text/email us at www.TellTheBell.com or 1-800-TacoBell or Text "TACO" to 91318. We would love to hear about your experience here at STORE #024556!!!*
> *ALSO GET LOCO WITH A DORITIO TACO. AND ENROLL IN THE CHANCE AT A FREE IPAD 2!!! :)*

Telling me, the customer, to tell you that "I love you, you are amazing, and your food is delicious" is an incredible turn-off and a huge customer service misstep. Any company that conveys this type of ask is making a lot of assumptions about their service.

How often do your clients miss the mark when seeking feedback? Do they ever state, "We ask our clients how they heard about us and none of them said TV?" Doesn't "heard" imply radio? Do they become defensive when feedback is negative? Maybe they refuse to believe responses, and as a result, miss an opportunity to move their business forward.

If you can believe it, my Taco Bell story is not over. It wasn't until about a mile down the road when the real disappointment of this detour surfaced. The drink was diet instead of the ordered regular and the two tacos were plain, despite my request for sour cream. Lastly, they must have been out of hot sauce because it never made it into the bag. I'm pretty sure the negative feedback I offered is exactly the kind of response that this particular Taco Bell owner was hoping to avoid.

CHAPTER 6

FOCUS ON YOUR CAREER

I've missed more than 9000 shots in my career. I've lost almost 300 games. 26 times I've been trusted to take the game-winning shot and missed. I've failed over and over and over again in my life and that is why I succeed. -Michael Jordan

THE REAL WORK BEGINS AFTER THE MEETING

When I managed television stations, the annual NAB Small Market Television Exchange (NAB SMTE) was always my absolute favorite industry event. The briefcase always got stuffed with extra paper and pens to take full advantage of the never-ending supply of sales ideas and executable thoughts. Plus, seeing my new broadcasting friends every year was like a mini-reunion.

After the convention, on the plane headed home, I would prioritize the volumes of notes. The intention was to organize the *most* important notes for fast implementation into our media operation. That was the *intention*.

Does this ever happen to you? Monday: You get back to the office after a few days of being away and you're met with a rush of updates from key employees. You work through a six-inch stack of mail, and then begin to return emails and phone messages. In the middle of these tasks, the LSM interrupts for an emergency meeting to discuss the resignation she just received from your star account executive. Tuesday: Your convention notes get pushed aside, thanks to a corporate request for a reforecast of the current quarter. On top of that, the NSM needs you to accompany him on a flight to Chicago before the end of the week to make amends with a buyer who just zipped your station on the quarterly buy. The days turn into weeks and the weeks into months.

Fast-forward to four months later when you decide your office needs a spring-cleaning. "What's this? Oh, that folder from the NAB conference with all my notes. I totally forgot about this!"

Great managers are great because they take action. But in order to take action, they have to have a plan. Today, I'm going to help you with your plan. You need to make an accountability contract with yourself. Likely, what I'm suggesting is no surprise to you, and you might already use it with your AE's after a multi-day training event. It's an idea worth reviewing and is worthy of doing to help you take full advantage of the great ideas you want to implement.

Creating A Personal Accountability Contract

Pick *five* of the best ideas from the conference that you'd like to adopt. Then prioritize in order: 1) something you can do tomorrow; 2) *two* things you will do next week, and finally; 3) *two* things you will add the following week. That's it. *Five* items. Lastly, sign and date the contract. Post or hang it somewhere in your office where you cannot help but see it multiple times a day. Please note that I suggest "post or hang"—not place in a file folder to be forgotten.

From personal experience, completing this accountability exercise produces *more* than *five* positive outcomes. The sense of accomplishment and positive momentum sprout new ideas and provide renewed energy for more action. That's when an average manager becomes great!

A Personal Contract

I, _____, hold myself accountable for adopting the following (as habits) in an effort to enhance my sales management abilities and to maximize my contribution to the *team*:

Tomorrow

1. _____

The Week of (one week out)

    1. _____

    2. _____

The Week of (two weeks out)

    1. _____

    2. _____

Signed _____ Date _____

****

ACTIVATE YOUR MINDSET SWITCH

Think of a competitor you envy. You know the one. They're typically the first in the market with new client offerings. They seem to effortlessly convert client dollars into new product revenue. They're able to pull money from client budgets that you didn't know existed. In short, their sales team could sell ice to an Eskimo.

In my travels, I've picked up on a consistent but very disturbing message in our industry. Apparently, some of your AE's and managers are under the impression that selling all of the company's offerings isn't possible. "How can corporate expect us to deliver revenue on our primary signal, our dot two station, digital and mobile products, and our quarterly projects?" they ask.

The answer is right between their ears but they have yet to hit the switch. The company you envy enjoys sales success because they have discovered how to activate the switch and change their mindset. A successful sales team celebrates the addition of new products. They are excited about the new "sales opportunities." They perceive the additions as, "Wow, look at the extra tools in our sales tool box. A hammer (dot two station) may not be the proper tool to help this client, but a screwdriver (digital platform) is the perfect tool!"

Don't spend time complaining about what you don't have, what the other companies do have, and ultimately, when you do get it how you cannot sell it.

The key to additional revenue is between your ears. All you have to do is activate the switch to change your mindset.

Are You Preparing Your Replacement?

This is a topic that gets little attention, but is one that seems to be fairly common and of quiet concern. As an industry, we do a poor job of mentoring and training replacements. My basis for making this statement is prompted by input from all levels of management across the country. Of course, there are exceptions.

First, let's discuss the major benefit of preparing someone to fill your shoes—opportunity for you.

Sure, naysayers will counter that there's a job loss threat if you have someone in-house ready to fill your spot. I contend that if that's your attitude, you could be clipped for any number of reasons, without training a replacement. Spending time with, mentoring, and helping standout performers progress their upward mobility career goals only makes your teams stronger. Selling up and positioning individuals as ready to lead places you in a position to be elevated to the next level because you have a management succession plan.

Preparing an Account Executive to be a Local Sales Manager. Many times, we award an LSM title to one of the sales staff's highest billing AE's. Sure, they've proven they can sell, but can they motivate the team to consistently sell at higher levels? Consider a few of these grooming steps before you give an AE an LSM promotion:

- Assign sales staff projects (plan and direct a client upfront party, make responsible for management of station sports sales, etc.).
- Have them lead a staff ratings book break-out.
- Announce the AE as the fill-in for a vacationing or traveling LSM.
- LSM's should periodically include their heir apparent on major local negotiations to allow them to get a feel for clients not on their list.
- Encourage the AE to serve on local advertising

club boards.

- Look for sales staff leadership opportunities for the AE to help transition their eventual move from sales peer to sales boss.

Preparing an Account Executive to be a National Sales Manager. Too often, the first time a new NSM sees a rep office is right after they've been promoted. That is not the best transition for a new NSM.

- GSM's should take the future NSM on a national trip and explain thoroughly the in's and out's of a rep office.
- Talk about who (rep firm or station) pays for what (cabs, meals, etc.) on national trips.
- Discuss the rep firm organizational chart and the firm's connection to the few remaining owners.
- Let the AE fill in for a vacationing or traveling NSM.
- Make sure the AE is the best at discussing ratings, shares, demos, CPP's and their application to your station.
- Have them guest-write the weekly NSM newsletter. (If your station is not writing one, you should be!)

Preparing an LSM and NSM to be a General Sales Manager. The key here is exposure to both sides of the sales house before becoming a GSM. As

149

a station General Manager, I once flipped the LSM and NSM in an effort to prepare both for the next step to GSM. That one move took the station from having *zero* to *two* in-house GSM candidates.

- GSM's should work with managers to make them experts in inventory management. Effective inventory management can be the difference between making or missing budget.
- LSM's should be on local calls every day. However, consider setting a minimum number of weekly appointments where the NSM has to ride with AE's. This continues to establish the NSM as a staff leader and keeps them in the loop with local decision makers.
- Likewise, take the LSM on a few national trips for the much needed exposure to rep players and buyers before a GSM promotion.
- Train on the responsibilities of a department head.
- Rehearse budgeting and expense scenarios.

Preparing a GSM to be a General Manager. GM's should seek out leadership opportunities for the GSM to gain the confidence of the entire station staff. If the GSM has the respect of the staff, his/her promotion to GM will not be a surprise and will be a welcomed transition.

- Explain the GM's report card: cash flow. This can sometimes be a foreign concept to a GSM's day-to-day, percent-to-budget measurement.

- Allow the GSM to sit in on syndicated pitches to help escalate understanding and relationships post-GM promotion.
- Review negotiations on news talent or union contracts.
- Consider having the GSM sit in quietly on a few GM conference calls to get a feel for corporate discussion.
- Have the GSM accompany station engineers to the transmitter for an education on equipment and digital sideband transmissions.
- Invite the GSM to community and civic meetings.

WHAT DO I DO WITH ALL OF THESE SUBSCRIPTIONS?

As a manager, you probably have a multitude of magazines, newsletters, and periodicals at your disposal. Upon ordering each, your intent was to read every word cover to cover. It's likely you planned to circulate the writings to the benefit of the staff. Armed with the latest sales improvement information, you envisioned yourself leading the sales team into never-before-seen revenue highs. That's a perfectly thought-out plan, but probably not reality.

Because of more pressing priorities, you no longer read cover to cover, or read the full length of email newsletters. You circulate items without looking at them, and your sales team, being short on time themselves, will sign off on magazines and periodicals as "read" and will delete your newsletter email forwards without reviewing. The whole process has become a mockery of your best intentions.

If the preceding describes you, a discussion of new ways to maximize the value of your subscriptions may be in order.

Begin by putting together a "to go" folder that fills the wasted minutes waiting on clients, sitting in airports, lunching by yourself, etc. In this folder, you'll put all of the reading you couldn't complete in the office.

- Scan titles and headlines for points of interest pertinent to aiding your team's sales effort or for addressing your clients' needs.
- Print, highlight, clip or forward email sections specifically for distribution to sales managers, department heads or sellers.
- Post smaller highlights or notes on the sales training or conference room bulletin board. Take the posts down and replace often so sales pros check back for fresh motivation.
- Clip an article for an AE and handwrite, "I thought this might help in your presentation, relationship, etc., with XYZ client."
- Clip and mail an article as a deposit to one of your station's key clients. After all, you cannot

make a withdrawal without making a deposit. A note from a manager to a client is huge!

- Manage up by clipping an article for your boss. Don't forget to use the margin to handwrite your thoughts for execution of the idea.

No doubt, there are many other unique and profitable ways to utilize your periodicals, newsletters, and magazines.

SAYING YES BEFORE YOU SAY NO

If you're a television or cable general manager, or aspire to be one, you understand the importance and incredible responsibility of being the keeper of the company checkbook. It's so important, that most compensation plans for managers at this level are tied to the ability to balance and adjust expenses based upon the inflow of revenue. In simple terms, this is cash flow. Given this information, it's easy to understand why many managers are stingy with the dollars.

I was reminded of this while listening to a sales manager's frustration over his GM never approving any purchase requests. My sales manager friend stated, "My GM always says no before he says yes."

Does this sound like anyone you know? Do you remember a time when someone may have said to you, "Before you say NO, please take a look at…?" In retrospect, when running stations there were times when managers in the building would likely have said the same about me. There are no excuses other than it was easier to dismiss the notion of spending the money. Many times, the thought of listening to a justification on the investment seemed to be wasted time.

Are there ever missed opportunities in these conversations? Would the News ratings increase with a graphics change? Could commercial rates increase with inventory management software? Would your account executives close more business after a sales training webinar?

Over time, I learned there are legitimate purchase "asks" that deserve attention. That's when I adopted a philosophy of "Yes." As in, "Yes, now that you've explained it, I do see we need to make a change. But, this is way out of the budget. Can you do a bit of research and find a cheaper alternative to fix this issue?" Again, this is for legitimate purchases. Saying yes before you say no, minimizes lost opportunities and creates an office of bargain shoppers, which helps you keep a rein on the checkbook. (Note: Sometimes engineers can really push the limits. The trump question with engineers is: "Will we go off the air unless we buy X?" If the answer is "no," then don't spend the money!)

This same lesson of saying yes before saying no applies to your AE's as well. Conditioning them to respond "yes" before an explanation will keep the conversation positive and will make the client feel the AE is trying to accommodate the request. For example, the client wants to pay $500 for a commercial in your highest rated prime show. The going rate is somewhere around $850. The majority of AE's would respond, "No. My manager would never approve that rate." (Although, some AE's might take the money and run, and then worry about pre-empts later!) Instead, sellers should respond in the affirmative with something like, "Yes, we can work with the $500 if your commercial is a fifteen-second copy." Or, "We can get a thirty-second in the break five minutes before the show. Which do you prefer?" If the client still wants the show, you then have a conversation about the rate it will take to clear.

Please remember, I'm not advocating saying "yes" to every question. What I am suggesting is that you replace knee jerk "no's" with a "yes." Doing so puts the requestor at ease and makes them feel as though you're working for an alternative in their best interest.

HIRE SELLERS WHO BUY LOTTERY TICKETS

Are you the type of person who participates in a Mega Millions lottery frenzy when there's a huge jackpot?

When big money is at stake, there are always a myriad of news reports, speculation stories and advice, and man-on-the-street interviews on what to do if you're the winner. I remember during one especially large jackpot approaching three-quarters of a billion dollars, there was an interview that caught my attention. The anchors threw the live broadcast to a reporter interviewing hopeful winners as they exited a local gas station which, of course, sold Mega Millions lottery tickets. The reporter stopped a Gen X female and asked, "You have a 1 in 259 million chance of winning the lottery jackpot. Why did you buy a lottery ticket?" The girl deadpanned into the camera, "Because I have a chance."

This young lady was obviously someone who looks at the glass as half-full. This got me thinking—how many of her friends expressed that she was wasting her money? How many countless times did she hear, "you're never going to win"? My guess is it's likely the same amount of times the actual winners heard the naysayers.

As a TV sales manager, do you ever feel like you're pushing the individual sellers or worse yet, the team, uphill? Are you sick of resistance every time you present a new opportunity for the sales tool box? Do you hear more "why we can't" than "why we can" comments?

Want the fix? Hire sellers who buy lottery tickets!

Please don't misunderstand me. I have zero scientific evidence that lottery ticket purchasers are great sellers. Certainly, there are many other variables that complete a great seller. However, it does stand to reason that optimists will perform better than pessimists in a career where rejection is commonplace.

Could it be that individuals who overlook seemingly insurmountable odds are more successful? Surely, in your sales career you have multiple stories about the new AE who closed (insert client), an account that all the Senior AE's on the staff said could never be sold. If the newbie would have listened to the *supposed* wiser Senior AE's, he/she might never have gone to see the client in the first place.

From my experience, sellers with a positive outlook carry themselves with confidence. This confidence is likely key to their ability to deliver more new business, a higher closing percentage, a "closer to the top of the rate card" unit average, and over-budget revenue highs.

So, maybe you might consider adding a lottery inquiry to your list of interview questions. It might help you understand the attitude of your next potential soon-to-be-sales star!

By the way, for that jackpot I bought 10 Mega Millions lottery tickets. Why not? I had a chance!

For you movie buffs:

Remember Jim Carey's character in *Dumb and Dumber*? He had a classic reaction when his hopeful love interest stated there was a one in a million chance they would date. His response? "So you're telling me there's a chance. Yeah!"

THREE STEPS TO TAPPING UNREALIZED POTENTIAL

A relatively new sales manager reached out for assistance in establishing new team goals. She was unsure where the bar should be set or what would be fair to her team. "That's easy," I told her. "Just make sure your team performs at never-before-experienced levels." She was understandably confused by my response until she understood the need to help sellers tap into their unrealized potential. Below are the three steps we discussed:

1) Ask "Why Not and What If?" Look at your team's goals. If done properly, you've incorporated a stretch in the goals but not anything that is impossible. Now, think beyond what you have established as the current goal(s). What does that look like? Does the view give you a little bit of apprehension? The only reason we limit our vision is because of our perceived capabilities. If you continue to think and operate the same way, you become stale and never realize your true potential.

If we thought of our potential without limits, how much further beyond our goals would we go? "Why not and what if" everyone on your sales team perfomed at this level? Current budgets would be shattered and new revenue records would be the norm. Asking "Why Not and What If?" creates a positive environment and turns problems into opportunity. But, nothing happens until you, as a leader, ask the question.

2) Set Goals That Do Not Exist. In our world of television sales, *setting goals that do not exist* takes courage. It's dreaming big. It takes a tremendous leader to get the team to buy into a big dream. Finish this sentence: "In a perfect world I would..." Doing so will establish your dream or a goal that does not exist.

As a TV station manager many years ago, I can recall my amazement in hearing stories of Edwin Hill, our Evansville sister station Vice President and General Manager. Year after year, this big-dreaming manager would go into the annual budget process proposing an aggressive double-digit revenue increase. After corporate gave their final number approval, Edwin would go to the sales staff and say something like, "Corporate *only* wants a 14% increase but I know we're capable of more. Let's talk about how we're going to deliver +19%!" Meanwhile, sister stations were trying to defend why their revenue increases should be *less than* 10%.

3) What will it take for your team to become the absolute best at what they do? To get your team to do things they've never done, they have to start doing things they've never done. Is your team driving with the brakes on? As a leader, it's up to you to establish and secure buy-in to the vision. What are the steps necessary to make your team the absolute best? Define the steps and encourage action.

In my last stop, as a TV General Manager, our statement to be the best was easily defined. We committed to being the best 1) in the market, 2) in the group, and 3) nationwide. Our department heads defined steps that would help us fulfill each of our commitments in order. Every employee had a business plan and goals, which rolled up into department goals. The department goals then supported the vision and goals for the station.

The most important thing to remember is that nothing happens until YOU make the choice to be the absolute best and your team believes that under your management, and ultimately your leadership, the seemingly impossible is absolutely possible.

YOU FIND WHAT YOU'RE LOOKING FOR

Randy Watson, a star TV sales pro at our long-time partner station WTHR, reached out after reading a blog I wrote on the importance of substituting positive words in place of negative language (www.jimdoyle.com/blog). Reading it reminded him of a great piece shared by peak performance coach and author, Brian Cain (www.briancain.com):

A man sat on a park bench when a traveler stopped by and asked, "What are the people like in this city?"

The man on the bench replied, "What are the people like where you came from?"

The traveler said, "They were a horrible bunch—mean, backstabbing and rude."

The man sat up on the bench, looked the traveler in the eye and said, "You will find the same people here in this city."

About an hour later, a second traveler approached the man on the bench and asked, "What are the people like in this city?"

The man on the bench replied, "What are the people like where you came from?"

The second traveler said, "They were wonderful. The nicest, warm and welcoming bunch you would ever find. It is so hard to leave, but my job takes me here."

The man sat up on the bench, looked the traveler in the eye and said, "You will find the same people here in this city."

The moral of the story is that you will find what you are looking for. If you're looking for negativity, you will find it; if you're looking for positivity, you will find it.

CHANGE YOUR LICENSE PLATES

In the media line of work, it's not uncommon to find

yourself in the middle of a job relocation. Maybe you're offered an opportunity to grow your career, so you embrace it and accept the out-of-town position that gets you a step closer to fulfilling your professional goals. Or, through no fault of your own, you find yourself in a new state, in a new management role, with a new company as a result of a station or outlet sale.

Congratulations! Now go change your license plates!

I'm serious.

Regardless of the stimulus behind your management move, understand and don't overlook that you may not be the only one trying to adjust to the change. As you begin to try to match AE names and faces, they are, at the same time, observing and judging you.

They're comparing you to their last manager, trying to get a handle on your accountability expectations, your leadership ability, your communications skills, your love of a good joke, your favorite teams, how you dress, how fast you walk, your organizational skills, and most importantly, your commitment level. That's where the license plates come into play.

Not too long ago, I caught up with a general manager friend over lunch. When he turned into the restaurant parking lot, I noticed that he still had out-of-state license plates on his car. The reason it was a surprise to me was that he'd accepted this cross country management move nearly *nine* months earlier. Yet, he was still driving around displaying his out-of-state plates.

During lunch, my friend revealed to me that there was a pocket of employees at the station who seemed less than enthusiastic to accept him as their station manager. These were good employees. They didn't display any disrespect, but for some reason there seemed to be an air of hesitation with the management change.

"Isn't it true that sometimes more information is conveyed in what *isn't* said vs. information from what *is* said?" I asked.

"Sometimes..." my friend hesitated, trying to guess my point.

I explained that some employees may feel that he, as their less-than-a-year new manager, may not be totally committed to staying in his new role. As a result, they may be hesitant to accept or get close to him for fear he may be leaving.

My friend responded that there was *no way* that could be possible. He had freely shared that he was looking for a new house and that he'd arrived expecting to be at the station for the long haul.

"Maybe so. At least that's what you've told them," I explained. "But the *unspoken* information being conveyed is that you're keeping your options open and are ready to move back to your home state if this new gig doesn't work out."

"Where would my employees ever get an idea like that?" my agitated friend replied.

"From looking at your car every day to see if you've changed your out-of-state license plates," I answered.

My friend sat silently letting the information sink in, and then finally admitted there may be some truth in our conversation. In the end, he promised a post-lunch drive to the DMV to get his new home state's license plates.

WHEN WAS THE LAST TIME YOU TOOK A TRUE VACATION?

It's always enjoyable looking at social media pictures of friends and their families enjoying some much deserved vacation time. But the pictures make me wonder how many of my career friends' smiling pictures give way to emails and work catch-ups late in the evening, while the family sleeps. Isn't time away from the office supposed to be time to recharge mental batteries?

When was the last time you took a true vacation? I mean, a full week or more of down-time, when business didn't interrupt your pleasure? We're talking about time off where you leave the office cell phone in your room to avoid business rings and email dings? If you can't remember, maybe you should be looking at booking that much needed vacation.

Most media managers I know feel they must call the office *daily* while vacationing. Thoughts of pacing, ratings, program changes, and personnel issues occupy their minds. It's almost as if they think business will come to a halt unless they hear the voices of productivity on the other end of the line. Sound familiar?

In the interest of full-disclosure, I used to be like those managers. A long time ago, as a television station GM on a client incentive trip, I called the station 3 to 4 times a day. The report was always the same, "Everything's fine. A few more orders have come in. We're still on the air." It was about the third day of this pace that one of our station sales managers grew tired of my calls. Before I could ask the status questions, she blurted out, "What more could I possibly tell you about the state of sales? You're entertaining two dozen of our top clients!" We both laughed at the absurdity and truth of that statement.

Do yourself, your employees, and your family a favor and stop calling and/or emailing the office while you're on vacation. Everyone knows how to reach you if there's an emergency. You honor employees and assist in their growth by allowing them the opportunity to live up to their titles and... your family will thank you.

I'm approaching the back third of my career. That sounds kind of funny coming from a guy that, as of this writing, is only 48 years old. But thankfully, I don't mean the back third in terms of age. No, this back third reference is in terms of thinking.

Remember your post-college job hunt? You were trying to get your foot into any media outlet that cracked their door open to take a look at you. Money wasn't the issue, getting the job was the priority because you knew in this first phase of career thinking, if only you were given the opportunity you were going to perform and the money would follow.

In the second phase of career thinking, many times we're burning the candle at both ends, trying to outperform peers to get the promotions, the titles, the money, and the increased responsibility to make decisions to affect change. Typically, this is the period of biggest life maturation, as we're working just as hard to raise a family and provide our kids a foundation of success.

In the back third of career thinking, I have discovered that while money is still important, the priorities begin to shuffle a bit. Life now isn't so much about the climb, it's more about the give back, the legacy. The legacy is not a personal one or focusing on how people remember John Hannon. Instead, it's how can I be better for those around me now, so that ultimately I can have a positive impact on the future of those who will one day be walking these hallways?

Where are you in your career thinking? More importantly, where are your team members in their career thinking? If you don't know, now might be a great time for you, as the leader, to ask. It's likely a question your sellers have rarely if ever heard and it might just be the spark of attention that brings you closer and kindles a mentorship.

THE FINAL LESSON

MANAGEMENT BY WALKING AROUND

A sales manager called to ask my input on something his _new_ general manager was doing. Apparently, the GM would, unannounced, walk into offices, cubical spaces, the news set, the lunch room, master control or anywhere there was a station employee—and just start a conversation.

"Are the conversations with the GM unpleasant?" I asked.

"No," the sales manager responded. "The encounters are quite the opposite. He asks about family, kids, and weekend plans. He wants to know what we're working on and if there's anything he can do to help."

"Ah, classic MBWA. You've got a great GM there," I said.

"MWB what?" the sales manager asked.

Very quickly I realized that **Management By Walking Around** (MBWA) was a foreign concept to this 20-year-plus, industry veteran. In fact, his previous long-time GM was quite the opposite—way on the other side of the spectrum—as in rear-end velcroed to a chair that was screwed to the floor under a nailed down desk. As a result, the encounters between the previous GM and employees were rare, and when they did happen, it was because there was an emergency or revenue was pacing way off the mark. The discussions were usually unpleasant. Given that information, I understood why the sales manager was a bit taken aback by the new GM's pleasant approach.

Throughout the series of *Engaged Management* books, I offer many techniques, tips, and examples to help you develop teams that accomplish never-before-realized levels of performance.

But, I've been holding out on you and it's time for full disclosure.

It is my belief that you can be extremely successful without practicing anything in the previous pages of this book.

Do you want to know the secret?

Get up right now and go walk the hallways of your office. Stop the first employee you see and start a conversation. Look them in the eyes. Make them feel special. Ask them things about their family, their interests, and their work projects. When the conversation is over, go find another employee and start another conversation. It really is that simple.

Star managers understand the value of checking in and taking temperatures through MBWA. They possess a curiosity that seals a bond, a connection, a positive and supportive culture that is ripe with "team" and "we're in this together." Very simply put, these successful leaders take an interest in their team members. They are present in the moment and always striving to practice engaged management, which is fundamental to *maximizing your team's sales performance.*

ABOUT THE AUTHOR

John Hannon is President of Jim Doyle & Associates, a marketing firm of speakers, authors, trainers, and consultants dedicated to helping television sales organizations consistently deliver positive revenue momentum.

John travels the country as an in-demand industry speaker. He works with television companies to develop profitable strategies for both media outlets and client advertisers. His extensive knowledge of television management, marketing, digital convergence, and sales enables him to help industry leaders create powerful selling cultures to significantly grow their businesses.

His broadcasting career began at the age of fifteen as a radio station disc jockey. By the age of eighteen, John answered the call of customer service as an account executive.

He offers clients an impressive portfolio of experience, having held various sales, station management, program distribution, and corporate positions with Tri-Radio Broadcasting, ACT III,

Sullivan Broadcasting, Sinclair Broadcasting, Quorum Broadcasting, and Acme Communications.

Under John's leadership, television stations have won five #1 in the nation awards, the network Model For Success, the Better Business Bureau Integrity Award, and multiple National Association of Broadcasting Sales Promotion awards.

John is a best-selling author. The first volume in his *Engaged Management* book series, *Inspiring Your Team To Win* was an Amazon #1 new release and a #1 best-seller in the category of Management & Leadership Training.

Originally from Ironton Ohio, John holds degrees from Central Texas College and Ohio University. He completed his Master's degree in Journalism and Broadcast Station Management at Marshall University. He is a member of the National Speakers Association.

John is a nearly twelve-year veteran of the Air Force, Air Force Reserve, and Army National Guard. He is a retired rugby player living in Sarasota, Florida, with wife Bridget, two daughters, a son, and two dogs.

EXPERIENCE
DOYLE ON DEMAND

The Television Industry's Premier Sales Training Platform

A multi-million dollar virtual interactive sales training platform, with 24/7 access via mobile, tablet, computer or any electronic device that has access to the Internet.

For the rookie seeking that first sale to sales veterans looking for new revenue highs to managers and leaders bent on building the best sales organizations in the industry, Doyle on Demand offers multiple interactive training courses and chapters designed to make you money and make you better.

THE LEADERS EDGE
COACHING PROGRAM

Let's face it. Our business is getting more difficult and complex every day. Change is occurring at the speed of light and it's your job to develop strategies and tactics and, even more importantly, to motivate your team to capitalize on these changes and lead them to success.

But you can't do it alone! You need a leadership coach—more specifically, a PERSONAL leadership coach! THE LEADERS EDGE PROGRAM is just that... a comprehensive personal coaching program specifically designed for TV and Cable sales managers. If the *Engaged Management* series has made an impact on you, then you'll want to check out this ongoing, multi-formatted, real-world program that's guaranteed to help you become a stronger leader. And great sales organizations are the result of STRONG LEADERSHIP!

TO LEARN MORE ABOUT THE LEADERS EDGE COACHING PROGRAM:

Visit: www.jimdoyle.com/store-2
Email: info@jimdoyle.com
Call Us: 941-926-*SELL* (7355)

CONTACTS

John M. Hannon
Jim Doyle & Associates, Inc.
7711 Holiday Drive
Sarasota, FL 34231

941-926-7355
john@jimdoyle.com
www.jimdoyle.com
www.doyleondemand.com

 /johnhannonmedia

 /in/johnhannonmedia

 /johnhannonmedia

 @johnhannonmedia

 /JimDoyleandAssociates

 /company/jim-doyle-&-associates

 /TVJimDoyle

41545853R00109

Made in the USA
Middletown, DE
16 March 2017